POLICY AND PRACTICE IN HEALTH AND SOCIAL CARE
NUMBER TWENTY-FOUR

Risk and Resilience:
Global learning across the age span

POLICY AND PRACTICE IN HEALTH AND SOCIAL CARE

See www.dunedinacademicpress.co.uk for details of all our publications

POLICY AND PRACTICE IN HEALTH AND SOCIAL CARE
SERIES EDITORS
CHARLOTTE L. CLARKE AND CHARLOTTE PEARSON

Risk and Resilience: Global learning across the age span

Edited by

Charlotte L. Clarke
Head of School, School of Health in Social Science, University of Edinburgh

Sarah Rhynas
Alzheimer Scotland Post-Doctoral Fellow, School of Health in Social Science, University of Edinburgh

Matthias Schwannauer
Professor of Clinical Psychology, School of Health in Social Science, University of Edinburgh

and

Julie Taylor
Professor of Child Protection, School of Nursing, Institute of Clinical Science, University of Birmingham and Birmingham Children's Hospital NHS Foundation Trust

EDINBURGH ◆ LONDON

First published in 2017 by Dunedin Academic Press Ltd.
Head Office: Hudson House, 8 Albany Street, Edinburgh EH1 3QB
London Office: 352 Cromwell Tower, Barbican, London EC2Y 8NB

ISBNs:
978–1–78046–063–5 (Paperback)
978–1–78046–561–6 (ePub)
978–1–78046–562–3 (Kindle)

Shelfie

A **bundled** eBook edition is available
with the purchase of this print book.

CLEARLY PRINT YOUR NAME ABOVE IN UPPER CASE
Instructions to claim your eBook edition:
1. Download the Shelfie app for Android or iOS
2. Write your name in **UPPER CASE** above
3. Add your book in the Shelfie app
4. Download your eBook to any device

British Library Cataloguing in Publication Data
A catalogue record for this book is available from the British Library

Typeset by Makar Publishing Production, Edinburgh
Printed in Great Britain by CPI Antony Rowe

CONTENTS

CONTRIBUTOR BIOGRAPHIES

Ruth Bartlett (PhD) is an Associate Professor in Ageing and Health Research at the Faculty of Health Sciences, University of Southampton, UK. She has published academic work, led social research studies and supervises doctoral students in areas related to dementia care and citizenship, health activism, ageing and participatory methods.

Dympna Casey (RGN, BA, MA, PhD) is Professor of Nursing and College Vice Dean for Interprofessional Learning at the National University of Ireland Galway, and has a clinical background in care of older people. Her research interests include care of older people, dementia, self-management of chronic diseases and health promotion. She has extensive experience in leading collaborative interdisciplinary and interinstitutional research projects. She has a keen interest in promoting healthier lifestyles for older people (in particular, people with dementia) and in examining ways of building resilience and supporting and maintaining the health and functional capacity of older people.

Charlotte L. Clarke (RN, BA, MSc, PhD, DSocSci) is Professor and Head of the School of Health in Social Science, University of Edinburgh, UK. Her research and practice focus on the development of risk theory in promoting risk enablement for people living with dementia.

Ilse Eigelaar-Meets (BA, MPhil) is a sociologist and partner in a social research company called SOREASO in South Africa. She works as a researcher and project manager and has also been involved in lecturing at both pre- and post-graduate levels in sociology and research methodology.

David Harvey (BA, MLS, MEd) leads a team at the Alzheimer Society of Ontario, Canada, in public policy and programme development and also co-leads the brainXchange, a national service providing knowledge translation and exchange related to brain health. He has nurtured the development of self-directed networks in a variety of areas.

Kathy Hickman (BASc, MEd, CDET) is the Education Manager with the Alzheimer Society of Ontario. She supports local Alzheimer societies through design and training for programmes such as the 'First Link Learning' series and 'Taking Control of Our Lives' for people with dementia and their care partners.

Barbara Klein (PhD) is Professor for Organisation and Management in Social Work at Frankfurt University of Applied Sciences in Germany and coordinator of an Independent Living Centre. Her research focuses on assistive technologies and social robots in the healthcare sector.

Annika Taghizadeh Larsson (PhD) is a Senior Lecturer in Ageing and Later Life at the National Institute for the Study of Ageing and Later Life (NISAL) at Linköping University, Sweden, which is an interdisciplinary research institute focusing on the interplay among the cultural, social, health and technical aspects of ageing in a changing society. She is also linked to the Centre for Dementia Research (CEDER), which conducts social scientific and humanistic research around people living with dementia diseases. Her research comprises questions and issues at the intersection of social gerontology and disability studies.

Lisa Loiselle (MA) is Associate Director of Research for the Murray Alzheimer Research and Education Program (MAREP) at the University of Waterloo, Canada. She has expertise in engaging people living with dementia, authentic partnerships in dementia care, and participatory action research.

Sandra Marais (PhD) is a Sociologist and worked as a Senior Specialist Scientist at the South Africa Medical Research Council for fifteen years before she retired in 2013. She has published widely, with research topics that include quality of life of older people, teenage pregnancy and reproductive healthcare, alcohol abuse among

pregnant women and studies on fetal alcohol spectrum disorders.
Carrie McAiney (BA, MA, PhD) is Associate Professor in the Department of Psychiatry and Behavioural Neurosciences at McMaster University, Canada. She works collaboratively with people living with dementia and their care partners to find effective and meaningful ways to enhance care and the care experience.

Kathleen Murphy (RGN, BA, MSc, PhD) has a clinical background in older people's services and emergency department nursing, and she held posts at Clinical Nurse Manager level in both. For the last twenty-five years she has worked in nursing education firstly at Oxford Brookes University, UK and then at the National University of Ireland Galway, where she is currently Professor of Nursing. Her research interests are in care of older people, dementia and chronic disease management. Her studies have focused on quality of life of older people living in residential care and the community, dementia, advanced nursing practice and chronic disease.

Ann-Charlotte Nedlund (BA, MA, PhD) is a Lecturer of Politics and Policy Analysis in Ageing and Later Life at the National Institute for the Study of Ageing and Later Life (NISAL) and the Centre for Dementia Research (CEDER), Department of Social and Welfare Studies at Linköping University, Sweden. She is also affiliated to the Division of Healthcare Analysis and to Medical Education – Interprofessional Learning, both at Linköping University. She has initiated and is a coordinator of the International Research Network on Citizenship and Dementia. At CEDER she is a coordinator of the research group Citizenship and Dementia. Her research primarily concerns issues related to citizenship, legitimacy, democracy and the welfare system.

Eija Paavilainen (PhD) is Professor of Nursing Science, School of Health Sciences, University of Tampere, Finland. Since 2002, she also has held a research position at South Ostrobothnia Hospital District, and was Professorial Fellow, University of Tampere, Research Collegium (2011–2012). Her research projects concern families, family violence, child maltreatment and family risks. She has more than 200 scientific and other publications and is Editorial

Board Member for *Child Abuse Review* (2012–2017).

Caroline Poole (BA, PGDip) is a Social Consultant and Partner in a social research company called SOREASO in South Africa. She works as a Researcher and Project Manager and has been involved in development projects serving a broad range of clients and stakeholders.

Ethel Quayle is Reader in Clinical Psychology in the School of Health in Social Science, University of Edinburgh. Her area of research is risk and vulnerability in the online sexual abuse and exploitation of children.

Sarah Rhynas (RGN, BSc, MSc, PhD) is the Alzheimer Scotland Post-Doctoral Research Fellow at the School of Health in Social Science, University of Edinburgh, UK. Her interests include the discharge of those living with dementia from hospital and discharge to care home. She enjoys using qualitative, sociological and creative research approaches.

Matthias Schwannauer (MA DPsych, PhD, CPsychol, AFBPsS) is Professor of Clinical Psychology, School of Health in Social Science, and Director of the Research Centre for Applied Developmental Psychology at the University of Edinburgh, UK. Prior to his full-time academic employment, he worked as a Consultant Clinical Psychologist in NHS Child and Adolescent Mental Health in Glasgow and Edinburgh, where he still maintains clinical involvement.

Julie Taylor (RN, BSc, MSc, PhD, FRCN) is Professor of Child Protection, Institute of Clinical Sciences, University of Birmingham and Birmingham Children's Hospital NHS Foundation Trust, UK. Her research programme is centred on child maltreatment as a public health issue.

Elaine Wiersma (MA, PhD) is an Associate Professor with the Centre for Education and Research on Ageing and Health, Lakehead University, Canada. Her research focuses on citizenship and self-management in dementia.

CHAPTER 1

Advancing Risk and Resilience: Why is it so important?

Charlotte L. Clarke, Sarah Rhynas, Matthias Schwannauer and Julie Taylor

Charlotte L. Clarke, Sarah Rhynas, Matthias Schwannauer, University of Edinburgh and Julie Taylor, University of Birmingham

Introduction

This chapter identifies some of the seminal work in the field of risk and resilience and identifies key similarities and differences in the way the field has evolved and been applied with children and young people and with older adults. As such, it includes child protection, the impact of early trauma on experiences later in life, children and young people mental health, ageing and dementia.

The following concepts are at the forefront of our analyses, each with clear policy and practice implications:

❏ location of responsibility and risk expertise – highlighting the policy shift between societal and individual responsibility, and the challenge to the dominance of professionalised knowledge holders;

❏ human rights and citizenship – highlighting the tensions between the societal mandate to protect vulnerable citizens and the right to be protected, and the right to have freedoms protected;

❏ agency and independence – highlighting the complexity of maintaining self-agency and independence in circumstances in which others judge you to require protection.

There are then some fascinating and critical issues that these concepts raise. In this chapter we start to open up these issues and to varying degrees they are addressed by the wide range of chapters in this book. We find ourselves asking the following questions:

❑ How does the societal mandate (to protect the vulnerable and 'at risk') enable and disable the individual?

❑ Who assumes and relinquishes responsibility for protection and decision-making, and with what consequences?

❑ Is the promotion of autonomy necessarily irreconcilable with expectations to protect individuals?

❑ How are some 'risky' behaviours not only safe but essential to developing and maintaining autonomy and individual identity of self?

❑ What lifespan developmental and interpersonal processes promote self-agency and the understanding of others as autonomous?

Let us say this another way:

'My mum, while she still had some mental capacity, said to me: "So what if I go out. If I get lost, someone will help me home. If I walk in front of a bus so be it – let nature take its course." We put mum's physical safety ahead of her freedom. She is now in a care home. We felt we had no choice. ☹'

Words written in response to an Economic and Social Research Council (ESRC) press release about the research on risk and resilience (http://forum.alzheimers.org.uk/showthread.php?63715-Risk-averse-carers-hasten-dementia-decline; accessed 27 June 2016) and a poignant reminder of the enormous tensions experienced everyday by those marginalised in their decision-making by social and societal exclusion and those living and working with them. Of course infants and very young children are not developmentally capable of any decision-making, yet they still express clear needs and have significant rights. It is these kinds of tensions – at the intersection of risk, resilience, citizenship and human rights in society – that drive the focus of this book and create an opportunity to challenge and impact upon the daily lives of people living with exclusion.

Responsibility and expertise

Critical social science approaches to risk and uncertainty recognise causal attributions of risk as profoundly associated with power, authority and blame (Brown, 2014; van Loon, 2014). In the discourse of risk the perceived probability of negative outcomes is utilised to undermine the adaptive behaviours and decision-making of individuals (Gigerenzer, 2010). The *risk society* perspective conceptualises risks as manufactured by people and therefore the responsibility to mitigate those risks lies with people living within the society (Giddens, 2000). One example of this may be our ageing population – the outcome of industrialisation, social and health-care advance resulting in a challenge that is being addressed in communities around the world. Less an insurable, calculable risk (Beck, 1994), these constructions of risk challenge assumptions and understandings, finding sociological meaning in the process of decision-making and the personal meaningfulness of the outcomes (Zinn, 2009).

In a challenge to the assumed dominance of authoritative voices, there is increasing recognition that people are risk experts in their own right, exercised through self-management and what services can perceive to be 'non-compliance' or disguised compliance. However differentiating between strategies for self-management in the face of, say, an adverse health situation and attempts to conceal mistreatment are ever-present challenges for practitioners and policymakers as they seek to balance promotion of autonomy and protection. Zinn (2005) highlights this shift towards less objective views of risk, which take greater account of socially situated realities, and considers individual biography and sociocultural situations as a backdrop to decision-making and risk prioritisation. He suggests that sociocultural and structural contexts do not fully account for individual behaviour, and he highlights the value of biographical self-representation in understanding decision-making and attitudes towards risk across the lifespan. Without this biographical approach the identification of risks prioritises the values of certain people over those of others (Foucault, 2000), leading to risk becoming a potential political tool, imposing particular values and concerns through the governance of risk, and it becomes a moral imperative seeking to reduce or eliminate uncertainty and potential harm (Hadis, 2014). Beck (1992) conceptualises risk as constructed through communication, noting that rational assessment and decision-making about risk are rarely possible when risk is developed and realised through social interaction. The rational identification of risk undermines the agency of the person at the centre of that decision – impacting on their development, welfare, decision-making, ability to maintain or achieve independence and can result in profound consequences, including:

relocation into care and the protection of social services; heightened surveillance; restriction (or liberation) of freedoms; and, potentially, alterations to a physical and social environment. Irrespective of age this impacts on key developmental transitions and opportunities and invites us to address relational aspects of location of responsibility and risk expertise.

On being part of society

One lens through which risk and resilience can be explored is the concept of 'citizenship in practice' (Bartlett and O'Connor, 2010). In challenging traditional, exclusionary notions of citizenship based on narrow notions of personal rights and responsibilities, Bartlett and O'Connor expand citizenship to include 'social practice' on the basis of Prior *et al.*'s work in which 'individuals relate to other people, their communities and the state' (Prior *et al.*, 1995) and Barnes *et al.*'s (2004) notion of 'everyday talk and actions'. Taking this concept further we would argue that citizenship in practice for people who are marginalised is co-constructed through the everyday practices that take place between them and those around them as they negotiate daily risks and opportunities. Yet there is an inherently political aspect to citizenship, which concerns the positioning of people who experience exclusion as active and activist in the relationship of their lives with their communities and in seeking to uphold their human rights. It is therefore the intersections between these concepts of risk, rights and resilience that are of critical importance to the well-being of individuals in our societies.

Perception of being 'at risk' arises from assessment of a vulnerability in either the individual and/or their psychosocial and environmental circumstances. This impacts on perceptions of their welfare, decision-making and ability to develop, maintain or achieve independence. To be perceived to be vulnerable and at risk (whether by the individual, professional services, family or members of the public) can result in profound consequences including relocation into care (e.g. a care home or foster care) and the protection of social services – it results in heightened surveillance, restriction (or liberation) of freedoms and, potentially, alterations to a physical and social/family environment (which may be perceived as safer and more protective of well-being yet also incur some detriment). The very acknowledgement and recognition of risk by individuals then becomes part of the appraisal of their perceived capacity and independence. Vulnerability may be inherent and legitimised by legislation as in childhood (Daniel, 2010) or may be a label bestowed by a professional. Being identified as carrying specific vulnerabilities in terms of the individual's mental health and well-being, irrespective of age, significantly impacts negatively on key developmental transitions and opportunities.

While there is a substantial track record of investigation into developing resilience in children and young people, applying concepts of resilience to older people, especially those with mental health needs, is in its infancy and much contested. Hicks and Conner (2014) note some of the challenges in defining resilience in older people with successful ageing, productivity and health status often being prioritised at the expense of social factors. Furthermore the experiences of a lifetime become embroiled in the development of resilience (Windle, 2011) and this is often reflected in the resilience of older people. These definition difficulties extend to disability studies where the need to move away from ability-focused models of resilience has pointed to the development of more relationship-focused approaches, which highlight life events (Hutcheon and Lashewicz, 2014). The development of resilience in different groups and across the lifespan has therefore not been fully explored. Likewise the research into risk management in older age has received little application to date in the field of children and young people. The role of protection by the wider society can both enable and disable the individual, yet is used at times as an uncontested societal mandate.

Agency and independence

Professional practice is profoundly shaped by the way in which policy and services engage with risk construction and management (Heyman et al., 2010; Gigerenzer and Muir Grey, 2013). However it is a large and very diverse body of theory and research, and can lead to some of the major ethical challenges faced by practitioners and by individuals and their families as they seek to engage with services and regulations that do not reflect the complexity of individual and family needs (Daniel and Bowes, 2011). Risk and resilience are identified as important concepts throughout the lifespan, yet there is little theoretical engagement with the concepts that take in the full spectrum of a lifetime. From a developmentalist's perspective, risk and adaptation to adverse circumstances not only foster autonomy and independence in early life but also define resilience on a collective and individual level. Family and community provides the safe haven from which individuals become competent agents and problem solvers. This process of adaptation and building resilience and autonomy continues throughout the lifespan and includes our relationship with societal structures, help seeking and the engagement with institutions. Johnson *et al.* (2010) reviewed literature across the lifespan, reporting a paucity of material and exploring the contrasts and continuities between literature on abuse across the life course. Their review highlights the difficulties arising from structures, services and academic thinking which are fragmented across a lifetime, preventing the development of either cohesive theory or research-informed policy and practice. Furthermore the dynamic nature of relationships within and between generations means that individuals view their own situations differently over time, and this may alter engagement with services and the appropriateness of those services (Bowes and Daniel, 2010).

These dynamics of theory, policy and practice have a profound influence on the experiences of people, and demand further analysis, greater continuity and potentially a reconsideration of legislation (Daniel and Bowes, 2011) and risk conceptualisation if we are to better enable individuals to live positively. Interest in the protection of vulnerable adults has brought into focus the need to revisit the assumptions underlying child protection systems (Daniel, 2010), perhaps highlighting the potential opportunity that a lifespan approach affords.

Risk is used to promote safety and is also, and in contradiction, used to promote autonomy. The perpetual tension between these uses of risk is manifest in accounts of people seeking to maintain their well-being and in the desire to maintain independence, which can lead to engaging in 'risky' activities and in which others collude. It is through such sense-making processes that people rationalise their engagement with (potentially) health-harming activities.

Crucially we need to consider where the responsibility for the management of risk rests – who assumes or relinquishes responsibility for the balance of protecting safety and promoting autonomy (as found by Clarke *et al.*, 2010). This also involves a different level of risk literacy among professions and institutions that often confuse actual risk and relative risk and use probabilistic heuristic methods (or rule of thumb) to make absolute decisions (Gigerenzer and Muir Grey, 2013). Powell *et al.* (2007) identify how risk theory enables an understanding of how people are rendered 'subjects' of society: 'risk is the intended outcome of a range of social practices whose aim is the management of a population that is useful, productive and self-managing' (Powell *et al.*, 2007, p. 73). Thus notions of voluntariness in the acquisition or relinquishing of responsibility for safety and autonomy are key to understanding the dynamics of relationships between an individual, their family and service providers. The confused position of responsibility is highlighted in policy too. People are however risk experts in their own right, which they exercise through self-management and what services can perceive to be 'non-compliance'. That this may be enacted with malign intent to obscure or obstruct identification of harm is central to the decision-making of practitioners and wider society too.

Risk theory, perception and management are central to concepts of choice and the capacity to execute decisions. It is essential to achieve the therapeutic benefit of optimal risk engagement and to recognise that the risk experiences of an individual are shaped by social and cultural forces across the globe – and are fundamentally shaped by the relationship between individuals, institutions and society (Lupton, 2013). This intersects with the emerging public health focus on prevention through promoting resilience in individuals (Garcia-Dia *et al.*, 2013) and forms a further aspect of the individualisation of responsibility. There are also considerations in terms of resilience education for professionals who are increasingly asked to support and foster resilience in their clients (Jacelon, 1997; Gilligan, 2008), extending to work on the development of resilience in the professionals themselves (Garcia-Dia *et al.*, 2013).

Protection and autonomy

Contemporary policies, which aim to empower people with choices and resources, represent a move away from earlier ideas in which risk was understood as something to be controlled and limited (and residing with the individual) rather than risk offering the opportunity to be beneficial to the individual (and residing in the context and circumstances surrounding the individual) (Adams, 2010). This move from managing 'vulnerable people' (through an emphasis on safety and loss) to managing vulnerable situations is evident in the contemporary language used, such as 'risk enablement', 'positive risk taking', 'reasonable risk' and positive risk in practice models. The emerging narrative focusing on the strengths and abilities of people is an uneasy companion with the narrative of vulnerability and protection, as well as a concern with litigation. For family members and professionals there can be real tension between wanting to avoid harm and wishing to uphold a person's autonomy (Robinson *et al.*, 2007; Clarke *et al.*, 2009; 2010).

The 'ethic of care' (Tronto, 1993; Sevenhuijsen, 2003) is a five-staged framework (attentiveness, responsibility, competence, responsiveness and trust), which provides a framework for considering the complexities of interpersonal relationships within the context of caring relationships. An 'ethic of care' shifts the focus away from traditional perceptions of care as one way and patronising, acknowledging the complexities of relationships and positioning care as political and moral, and it promotes citizenship in the context of interdependent relationships (Barnes, 2012). Applied to people with dementia, an ethic of care also balances the tension between independence, control and choice and the need of many people accessing services for care. It values the participation of all people involved, thus promoting citizenship in the context of care, acknowledging that some people are unable to 'care' for themselves, but that an ethic-of-care approach can enable voices to be heard, leading to participation (Brannelly, 2011).

Research challenges

In bringing citizenship of those who are marginalised and excluded into the research process itself, we as researchers are required to have a heightened level of reflexivity and an understanding of knowledge as a provocateur which exists in wicked environments with multiple, contradictory viewpoints – and creating meaning which Denzin and Lincoln (2003) describe as 'radically pleural, always open'. As such, the participatory approaches engage with a range of stakeholders and create a space for dialogue with those voices most often marginalised and silenced by the dominant presence and understandings of researchers. Achieving this requires the intimate engagement of stakeholders themselves in the research process (Somekh, 2002) and the creation of the collaborative project, which 'joins the researcher and researched in an ongoing moral dialogue' (Denzin and Lincoln, 2003). Opening up spaces for participants' voices to be heard requires researchers to consider how the research relationship and methodology facilitate this process, recognising how the methods used can reinforce researcher authority over the re/presentation of others' experiences (Richardson, 1990; Lather, 1991). Zinn's (2005) biographical approach to social research may offer strategies that allow researchers insights into an individual's experience, contextualised within their own biographical milestones, life course and identity.

A participatory (often arts-mediated) methodology challenges us to question whether the validity (or confirmability) of research is a property of the teller or the receiver. Participatory (and arts-mediated) methodologies provide the receiver with possibilities but leaves them free to interpret as they wish. For researchers however it demands that we suspend any search for a singular truth that is owned by ourselves, and instead focus attention on:

- reflexivity – the juxtaposition of self and subject matter;
- multiple voicing – the rejection of single, integrating conclusions;
- literary styling – the replacement of traditional realist discourse;
- performance – expanding communities in dialogue and avoiding claims of truth.

Overview of the book and chapters
We are delighted that the contributors to this book are drawn from around the world – colleagues who we have collaborated with,

often over several years, through the International Research Collaboration on Risk in Ageing Populations and, more recently, the International Interdisciplinary Research Group on Repositioning Risk and Resilience. This first chapter has sought to map out some of the complex societal issues of risk and resilience across the lifespan, and each of the other chapters offers a specific insight into work being undertaken in very varying societal contexts – each shedding a different light on issues of risk and resilience. Here we outline each chapter briefly.

In Chapter 2, Eija Paavilainen explores some of the consequences of child abuse and neglect and the challenges for practitioners working with families. Paavilainen highlights that myriad physical and other health problems can be a consequence of child abuse and neglect, and that families living with a risk situation may not attend welfare clinics and require particular attentiveness from staff to notice and address their concerns. Paavilainen argues that a risk assessment tool can be a useful part of a risk assessment process for staff.

In Chapter 3, Ruth Bartlett explores the multiple perspectives of risk for people with dementia who go outdoors – ranging from the risk of harm from becoming lost, to the risk of being confined at home or even having to move to a care home. Bartlett discusses the use of Global Positioning System (GPS) technologies as a way of creating a shared, or pooled, approach to responsibility. She highlights the sometimes controversial infringement of civil liberties and urges a prioritisation of the needs and rights of people with dementia themselves.

In Chapter 4, Elaine Wiersma and colleagues explore the consequences of dementia being located in narratives of risk and decline. They describe the development of a self-management programme to enhance adaptation and resilience, emphasising the key intertwining of structure and agency and the promotion of the social citizenship of people living with dementia.

In Chapter 5, Dympna Casey and Kathy Murphy discuss resilience and dementia, highlighting the therapeutic nihilism that has led to people with dementia being regarded historically as incompetent and without personhood. They explore resilience as the positive adaptation to major adversity and as a process, opening up a space in which assets and protective factors are important.

In Chapter 6, Ethel Quayle takes us on a journey through sexuality and agency in young people, with the Internet as a contested space. Quayle describes the changing nature of childhood, where children who have grown up with technology-mediated communication seem to make little distinction between the online and offline worlds. Children who are at risk or take risks in one world will echo this in the other. While exposure to risks online is fairly unavoidable, it is not inevitable that it will result in harm. Quayle argues how concerns about risks and harm to young people can detract from children's rights and agency.

In Chapter 7, Barbara Klein introduces us to three robots: the therapeutic seal PARO, the telepresent robot GIRAFF and the humanoid-like telepresent robot TELENOID. Discussed in the context of the growth of the care home sector and workforce in Germany, Klein uses the MEESTAR model to consider the ethical issues of using robots with older people and assesses each for its contribution to internal and external factors that confer resilience.

In Chapter 8, Sandra Marais and colleagues describe research they undertook in South Africa to address high rates of teenage pregnancy in two rural schools. Boys and girls had different views of love and sex, and girls were often left with the responsibility for contraception but without any power. The authors argue that interventions need to be multifaceted. Children and young people face multiple risk factors on the path to adulthood – the real challenge is to balance the promotion of autonomy while at the same time rendering protection.

In Chapter 9, Ann-Charlotte Nedlund and Annika *Taghizadeh* Larsson explore how to protect and also support people with dementia in enhancing citizenship. They focus their analysis on the legal framework in Sweden, where the right to self-determination is central to Swedish democracy. This leads to complex dilemmas in which someone with dementia cannot be declared incompetent in making decisions, yet do need some protections at time.

References

Adams, T. (2010) 'The social construction of risk by community psychiatric nurses and family carers for people with dementia.' *Health, Risk and Society*, Vol. 3, No. 3, pp. 307–19

Barnes, M. (2012) *Care in Everyday Life. An ethic of care in practice*, Bristol: Policy Press

Barnes, R., Auburn, T. and Lea, S. (2004) 'Citizenship in practice', *British Journal of Social Psychology*, Vol. 43, No. 2, pp. 187–206

Bartlett, R. and O'Connor, D. (2010) *Broadening the Dementia Debate: Towards social citizenship*, Bristol: Policy Press

Beck, U. (1992) *Risk Society: Towards a new modernity*, London: Sage

Beck, U. (1994) *Ecological Enlightenment: Essays on the politics of the risk society*, Atlantic Highlands, NJ: Humanities Press

Bowes, A. and Daniel, B. (2010) 'Interrogating harm and abuse: A lifespan approach', *Social Policy and Society*, Vol. 9, No. 2, pp. 221–9

Brannelly, T. (2011) 'That others matter: The moral achievement – care ethics and citizenship in practice with people with dementia', *Ethics and Social Welfare*, Vol. 5, No. 2, pp. 210–16

Brown, P. (2014) 'Risk and social theory: The legitimacy of risks and risk as a tool of legitimation', *Health, Risk and Society*, Vol. 16, No. 5, pp. 391–7. doi: 10.1080/13698575.2014.937678

Clarke, C. L., Gibb, C., Keady, J., Luce, A., Wilkinson, H., Williams, L. and Cook. A. (2009) 'Risk management dilemmas in dementia care: An organisational survey in three UK countries', *International Journal of Older People Nursing*, Vol. 4, pp. 89–96

Clarke, C. L., Keady, J., Wilkinson, H., Gibb, C., Luce, A., Cook, A. and Williams, L. (2010) 'Dementia and risk: Contested territories of everyday life', *Journal of Nursing and Healthcare in Chronic Illness*, Vol. 2, No. 2, pp. 102–12

Daniel, B. (2010) 'Concepts of adversity, risk, vulnerability and resilience: A discussion in the context of the "child protection system"', *Social Policy and Society*, Vol. 9,. No. 2, pp. 231–41

Daniel, B. and Bowes, A. (2011) 'Rethinking harm and abuse: Insights from a lifespan perspective', *British Journal of Social Work*, Vol. 41, pp. 820–36

Denzin N. K. and Lincoln Y. S. (2003) *Collecting and Interpreting Qualitative Materials*, Thousand Oaks, CA: Sage Publications

Foucault, M. (2000) 'The birth of social medicine', in Fabio, J. (ed.) (2000) *Essential Works of Michael Foucault – Volume 3 (Power)*, London: Penguin

Garcia-Dia, M. J., DiNapoli, J. M., Garcia-Ona, L., Jakubowski, R. and O'Flaherty, D. (2013) 'Concept analysis: Resilience', *Archives of Psychiatric Nursing*, Vol. 27, pp. 264–70

Giddens, A. (2000) *Risk in Runaway World*, London: Routledge, Chapter 2

Gigerenzer, G. (2010) *Rationality for Mortals: How people cope with uncertainty*, New York, NY: Oxford University Press

Gigerenzer, G. and Muir Grey, J. A. (2013) *Better Doctors, Better Patients, Better Decisions: Envisioning Health Care 2020*, Cambridge, MA: MIT Press

Gilligan, R. (2008) 'Promoting resilience in young people in long-term care: The relevance of roles and relationships in the domains of recreation and work', *Journal of Social Work*, Vol. 22, No. 1, pp. 37–50

Hadis, B. F. (2014) 'Risk, social protection and trust amidst cuts in welfare spending', *Health, Risk and Society*, Vol. 16, No. 5, pp. 459–80; doi: 10.1080/13698575.2014.936832

Heyman, B., Shaw, M., Alaszewski, A. and Titterton, M. (2010) *Risk, Safety, and Clinical Practice*, Oxford: Oxford University Press

Hicks, M. and Conner, N. E. (2014) 'Resilient ageing: A concept analysis', *Journal of Advanced Nursing*, vol. 70, No. 4, pp. 744–55

Hutcheon, E. and Lashewicz, B. (2014) 'Theorizing resilience: Critiquing and unbounding a marginalizing concept', *Disability and Society*, Vol. 29, No. 9, pp. 1383–97

Jacelon, C. S. (1997) 'The trait and process of resilience', *Journal of Advanced Nursing*, Vol. 25, pp. 123–9

Johnson, F., Hogg, J. and Daniel, B. (2010) 'Abuse and protection issues across the lifespan: Reviewing the literature', *Social Policy and Society*, Vol. 9, No. 2, pp. 291–304

Lather, P. (1991) *Getting Smart: Feminist Research and Pedagogy with/in the Postmodern*, New York, NY: Routledge

Lupton, D. (2013) *Risk*, London: Routledge, 2nd edn

Powell. J., Wahidin, A. and Zinn, J. (2007) 'Understanding risk and old age in western society', *International Journal of Sociology and Social Policy*, Vol. 27, pp. 65–76; doi: 10.1108/01443330710722760

Prior, D., Stewart, J. and Walsh, K. (1995). 'Opening up government', in *Citizenship: Rights, Community and Participation*. London: Pitman, Chapter 8

Richardson, L. (1990) *Writing Strategies: Reaching diverse audiences*, Newbury Park, CA: Sage

Robinson, L., Hutchings, D., Corner, L., Finch, T., Hughes, J., Brittain, K. and Bond, J. (2007) 'Balancing rights and risks: Conflicting perspectives in the management of wandering in dementia', *Health, Risk and Society*, Vol. 9, No. 4, pp. 389–406; doi: 10.1080/13698570701612774

Sevenhuijsen, S. (2003) 'The place of care: The relevance of the feminist ethic of care for social policy', *Feminist Theory*, Vol. 4, No. 2, pp. 179–97

Somekh, B. (2002) 'Inhabiting each other's castles: Towards knowledge and mutual growth through collaboration', in Day, C., Elliott, J., Somekh, B. and Winter, R. (2002) *Theory and Practice In Action Research*, Providence, RI: Symposium Books

Tronto, J. (1993) *Moral Boundaries: A political argument for an ethic of care*, London: Routledge

Van Loon, J. (2014) 'Remediating risk as matter–energy–information flows of avian influenza and BSE', *Health, Risk and Society*, Vol. 16, No. 5, pp. 444–58; doi: 10.1080/13698575.2014.936833

Windle, G. (2011) 'What is resilience? A review and concept analysis', *Reviews in Clinical Gerontology*, Vol. 21, No. 2, pp. 152–69; doi: 10/1017/S0959259810000420

Zinn, J. O. (2005) 'The biographical approach: A better way to understand behaviour in health and illness', *Health, Risk and Society*, Vol. 7, No. 1, pp. 1–9

Zinn, J. O. (2009) 'The sociology of risk and uncertainty: A response to Judith Green's "is it time for the sociology of health to abandon risk?"', *Health, Risk and Society*, Vol. 11, No. 6, pp. 509–26

CHAPTER 2

Assessing Child Maltreatment Risk in Families

Eija Paavilainen

Eija Paavilainen, University of Tampere, Finland

Introduction

Child maltreatment can be defined as the physical and emotional abuse and neglect of children. It also refers to living in a violent home – seeing violence between parents, for example. It is a global public health problem and a challenging issue for children and families themselves as well as for professionals in different fields who are trying to help them. Besides causing suffering for children and families, child maltreatment costs money for health and social services as well as child protection, thus impacting the entire society (see also Barlow *et al.*, 2007).

According to the systematic review of Norman *et al.* (2012), all forms of child maltreatment should be considered important risks to health, being major contributors to the burden of disease in all parts of the world. They found strong evidence of different forms of maltreatment in those suffering from depression and behavioural disorders, for example. According to Bair-Merritt *et al.* (2013), children have higher rates of myriad physical and other health problems in cases where they live with family violence. The health problems may be caused by their highly stressful environments. Early childhood represents the greatest period of vulnerability to stress-related changes in the brain, as tremendous brain growth occurs during this period. It has been determined that, every year, 4–16% of children are physically abused and one in ten is neglected or emotionally abused (Gilbert *et al.*, 2009). According to Taylor and Lazenbatt (2014), child maltreatment has not been effectively identified or prevented enough.

Child maltreatment should be identified and intervened in as early as possible, before a cycle of violence has been developed within the family. Risk factors for child maltreatment have been studied extensively, and we have researched evidence of risks concerning the child, parents and the family situation (Paavilainen and Flinck, 2013). Also tools for child maltreatment risk assessment and for the screening of child maltreatment have been developed and tested, especially to be used in emergency departments for finding physical abuse. However none of them has proved to be effective in all situations (Bailhache *et al.*, 2013). Still these tools remain useful for assessing the situations of children and families, as parts of assessments, during discussions with parents and children, during home visits, etc. (Paavilainen and Flinck, 2015). Through effective and useful risk assessment practices it is also possible to find the strengths of children and families, opening up spaces for the discussion with families and for opening their own voices (Chapter 1 in this book), and to support them, thus adding resilience to them. It is crucial to find ways to evaluate risks without labelling families.

The aim of this chapter is to describe child maltreatment risk assessment based on previous research evidence, to present one tested and useful tool for risk assessment and to discuss its potential for finding families at risk and then increasing their family resilience by supporting them.

Child maltreatment risk assessment

The identification of child maltreatment or the risk of child maltreatment is a process that starts from some kind of vague or strong suspicion or is one that is based on clear markers and symptoms. During the process, which can be quick or take a long time, maltreatment can be confirmed or remain open. For example, when there are clear physical markers on the child, the time needed can be quite short, and decisions about how to take care of the situation can be made quickly. Risk factors for child maltreatment from the viewpoints of the child, parents and the family situation are especially helpful in situations in which the markers are not so clear (Inkilä *et al.*, 2013; Leppäkoski *et al.*, 2014; Paavilainen *et al.*, 2014; Paavilainen and Flinck, 2015). However knowledge of risk factors should not be used for judging or blaming families. Rather, this knowledge should be adopted for assessing families' situations, which includes discussing especially the issues that seem to be child maltreatment risks.

According to Knoke and Trocmé (2005), accuracy in assessing risk is crucial in ensuring that appropriate decisions concerning the situation are made and that appropriate intervention is provided. Clinical experience and 'practice wisdom' have traditionally informed workers' service decisions. Good clinical skills are an integral part of the assessment process. However their sufficiency for making determinations about future maltreatment has been questioned. The value of more standardised approaches to risk assessment has been recognised, and a more systematic approach to the development and testing of risk assessment instruments is required to support child welfare practice and add to its quality.

In our study, we have aimed to increase the quality of risk assessment, and we used one broadly tested instrument – Child Abuse Potential (CAP) (Milner and Crouch, 2012) – for measuring the risk of child maltreatment within families expecting babies (Ellonen *et al.*, n.d.; Lepistö *et al.*, n.d.). During pregnancy (with thirty weeks as a baseline), some 380 families (360 mothers and 301 spouses) filled out questionnaires measuring risk (CAP) and family health, functioning and social support (FAFHES). This instrument has been developed for measuring functioning of families and support they receive from healthcare settings, in different situations. The instrument was modified for this study to be suitable for families expecting a baby (Paavilainen *et al.*, 2006) and was distributed at maternity clinics. In twenty families only spouses filled out the questionnaires. The aim of our follow-up study, which included the Supportive Discussion Intervention for families at risk and was conducted with families in the case group, was to find families at risk and then follow possible changes in the risk and family health and functioning when the baby reached about twelve months. In our study, we used CAP as the risk screening tool for the general population, meaning all pregnant families visiting maternity clinics, who wanted to participate in the study. Previously tools assessing child maltreatment had been mostly used within families with already known child maltreatment or within high-risk families, such as families with drug abuse, or with young, single mothers.

Of the families involved in the study, 89% were married or cohabitating, and 136 families were expecting their first babies. Seventy-eight families had child maltreatment risk: twelve of them with both parents and sixty-six with one parent. The mothers' risk level was a little higher than that of their spouses – slightly increased (n=10; 5%), increased (n=4; 2%) and strongly increased (n=2; 1%) (Ellonen *et al.*, n.d.; Lepistö *et al.*, n.d.). This is consistent with previous studies, even though measured by different risk evaluation instruments. According to Bailhache *et al.* (2013) all risk assessment instruments can be used only as a part of child maltreatment risk assessment. Some 7% of the mothers and 11% of the spouses said it was difficult for them to discuss family problems with others. Families at risk received less support from maternity clinics than did others (Ellonen *et al.*, n.d.; Lepistö *et al.*, n.d.).

Still we can conclude that families with child maltreatment risk were found in our study. The internal consistency of the abuse scale was high among mothers and spouses. The KR-20 reliability coefficient among mothers was 0.85 (n=368), and among spouses it was 0.80 (n=298) (Ellonen *et al.*, n.d.). Similar findings have been reported in other studies based on a translated version of the CAP (Milner and Crouch, 2012). Walker and Davies (2010), for example, reported, across Croatian, Greek and Spanish translations, internal consistency estimates ranging from 0.88 to 0.93 for general population and comparison parents and from 0.90 to 0.91 for maltreating parents.

Families living with a risk situation do not necessarily visit maternity and child welfare clinics regularly, or they might think that their problems are not being discussed properly. They might also feel they lack confidence about describing their situations well enough. The staff's skills in dealing with family risks and problems or the resources of multiprofessional care services may also be lacking. More specifically there might be a lack of services, or they might not be arranged in the best possible way. This may lead to situations in which families do not feel they are getting the support they would like from the staff members of the clinics they visit. Staff require risk assessment tools that are easy to use. They need joint guidelines on how to take care of children and families within multiprofessional teams, and training that helps them to address sensitive issues such as child maltreatment risk. According to Kanervio *et al.* (n.d.), public health nurses believe that they identify risks quite well based on their clinical expertise, training, work in teams and discussions with families. They also think a risk assessment tool such as CAP is a useful part of risk assessment. With this kind of tool it may be easier to start a discussion of a sensitive issue such as child maltreatment or risk of it. It is also helpful to say to the family that the tool is used with all families.

When using risks assessment tools such as CAP it is crucial to discuss with families the role of these tools. Families need to know that the aim is to help them to learn about and consider their situations based on the tools, as well as on discussions with the staff. A tool is a means of starting a discussion about a sensitive and difficult issue, both for families and for the public health nurses: for example, meeting all families that are expecting babies or living with children. The tools are just a basis and may be a starting point for the discussion. Risk assessment includes evidence-based knowledge (e.g. Paavilainen and Flinck, 2015), family and professional experience and sensations, and empathy and feelings. The ultimate aim is to increase the resilience and strengths of the family and children.

Conclusions

The early identification of families with child maltreatment risk is possible with CAP, according to the experiences of our study, and used as a part of discussing with families about their life situation. Supporting these families is also crucial and includes strengthening them within multiprofessional teams and treating the families themselves as active partners, having their own expertise concerning their own life. It is easier to support and help a family before the pattern of maltreatment has developed within the family, and before the family situation has lead to a crisis, such as the escalation of the violence.

Within the services of families and children, staff should be aware of, identify and discuss the family situations and risks. They should ask about child maltreatment and about family violence in general, and they should tell the parents how maltreatment and violence affect children. For that, they can use risk assessment tools such as CAP, which we have tested.

In Finland there is relatively good legislation concerning child protection and child maltreatment issues, and there is also a high-level service system for families with children. All children visit child welfare clinics, so it would be easy to use CAP for all families expecting babies. This could be one means to try to cut intergenerational child maltreatment within the family. However CAP needs to be tested more for clinical purposes. This may include filling the brief version (BCAP) (Ondersma *et al.*, 2005; Walker and Davies, 2012) during the family visit to the maternity clinic, assessing the risk by the public health nurse and, after that, discussing the result together. We will use the BCAP in our next research project during 2016–2018 (funded by the Ministry of Social Affairs and Health, Project 201,610,044), aiming to apply the instrument in clinical settings by all families (maternity and welfare clinics and hospital maternity wards). We will evaluate its efficiency and usefulness in clinical practice, as a tool for opening the discussion with families on their life situation and, for example, on their child-rearing practices. Some language modifications of the items may also be necessary to add the cultural understanding of CAP to Finnish families. While the translation of the items from English to Finnish has been made carefully, it is necessary to check them again.

We are trying to find better ways to achieve multiprofessional teamwork within and between different agencies, especially for exchanging information between professionals concerning children and families. In addition to exchanging information, it is important to concentrate on how to use the shared information. According to Munro (1999), the professional reasoning processes in child protection are not always clear. Errors in these processes can happen, but they can be reduced if people are aware of them and consciously strive to avoid them. Munro concludes that reasoning tools need to be developed to make them more rigorous and systematic. We also need to remember the weakness of human reasoning – the reluctance to change one's mind. As a result, families may easily stick with the results of family assessments that have already been done of their families. Especially when professionals receive new information that contradicts their views, it is hard for them to change their previous assessments. This idea should be more clearly included in different professionals' training.

References

Bailhache, M., Leroy, V., Pillet, P. and Salmi, L.-R. (2013) 'Is early detection of abused children possible?: A systematic review of the diagnostic accuracy of the identification of abused children', *BMC Pediatrics*, Vol. 13, p. 202. Available from URL: http://bmcpediatr.biomedcentral.com/articles/10.1186/1471-2431-13-202 (accessed 27 June 2016)

Bair-Merritt, M., Zuckerman, B., Augustyn, M. and Cronholm, P. (2013) 'Silent victims – An epidemic of childhood exposure to domestic violence', *The New England Journal of Medicine*, Vol. 369, No. 18, pp. 1673–5

Barlow, J., Davis, H., McIntosh, E., Jarrett, P., Mockford, C. and Stewart-Brown, S. (2007) 'Role of home visiting in improving parenting and health in families at risk of abuse and neglect: results of a multicentre randomised controlled trial and economic evaluation', *Archives in Diseases of*

Childhood, Vol. 92, pp. 229–33; doi: 10.1136/adc.2006.095117

Ellonen. N., Lepistö, S., Helminen, M. and Paavilainen, E. (In press) 'Cross-cultural validation of the child abuse potential inventory in Finland: Preliminary findings of the study among parents expecting a baby', Tutkiva Hoitotyö

Gilbert, R., Widom, K., Browne, K., Fergusson, D., Webb, E. and Janson, S. (2009) 'Burden and consequences of child maltreatment in high-income countries', *The Lancet*, Vol. 373, January, pp. 68–81.

Inkilä, J., Flinck, A., Luukkaala, T., Åstedt-Kurki, P. and Paavilainen, E. (2013) 'Interprofessional collaboration in the detection of and early intervention in child maltreatment', *Nursing Research and Practice*; doi: 10.1155/2013/186414

Kanervio, M., Kylmä, J. and Paavilainen, E. (n.d.) 'Public health nurses experiences concerning family risk assessment in maternity and child welfare clinics' (manuscript to be submitted)

Knoke, D. and Trocmé, N. (2005) 'Reviewing the evidence on assessing risk for child abuse and neglect', *Brief Treatment and Crisis Intervention*, Vol. 5, No. 3, pp. 310–27

Lepistö, S., Ellonen, N., Helminen, M. and Paavilainen, E. (n.d.) 'The family health, functioning, social support and child maltreatment risk of families expecting a baby' (manuscript accepted for publication in Journal of *Clinical Nursing*)

Leppäkoski, T., Flinck, A. and Paavilainen, E. (2014) 'Assessing and enhancing health care providers' response to domestic violence', *Nursing Research and Practice*; doi: 10.1155/2014/759682

Milner, J. and Crouch, J. (2012) 'Psychometric characteristics of translated versions of the child abuse potential inventory', *Psychology of Violence*, Vol. 2, No. 3, pp. 239–59

Munro, E. (1999) 'Common errors of reasoning in child protection work', *Child Abuse and Neglect*, Vol. 23, No. 8, pp. 745–58

Norman, R., Byambaa, M., De, R., Butchart, A., Scott, J. and Vos, T. (2012) 'The long-term health consequences of child physical abuse, emotional abuse, and neglect: A systematic review and meta-analysis', *PLOS Medicine*, Vol. 9, No. 11. Available from URL: http://journals.plos.org/plosmedicine/article?id=10.1371/journal.pmed.1001349 (accessed 27 June 2016)

Ondersma, S., Chaffin, M., Mullins, S. and LeBreton, J. (2005) 'A brief form of the child abuse potential inventory: Development and validation', *Journal of Clinical Child and Adolescent Psychology*, Vol. 34, No. 2, pp. 301–11

Paavilainen, E. and Flinck, A. (2013) 'National nursing guideline for identifying and intervening in child maltreatment in Finland', *Child Abuse Review*, Vol. 22, pp. 209–20

Paavilainen, E. and Flinck, A. (2015) 'Effective methods for identifying child maltreatment in social and health care' (online clinical guideline from Nursing Research Foundation). Available from URL: http://www.hotus.fi/system/files/SUOSITUS_lasten_kaltoinkohtelu_ENGLANTI%20%282%29.pdf (accessed 27 June 2016)

Paavilainen, E., Helminen, M., Flinck, A. and Lehtomäki, L. (2014) 'How public health nurses identify and intervene in child maltreatment based on the national clinical guideline', *Nursing Research and Practice*; doi: 10.1155/2014/425460

Paavilainen, E., Lehti, K., Åstedt-Kurki, P. and Tarkka, M.-T. (2006) 'Family functioning assessed by family members in Finnish families of heart patients', *European Journal of Cardiovascular Nursing*, Vol. 5, pp. 54–9

Taylor, J. and Lazenbatt, A. (2014) *Child Maltreatment and High Risk Families*, Protecting Children and Young People series, Edinburgh: Dunedin Academic Press

Walker, C. and Davies, J. (2010) 'A critical review of the psychometric evidence base of the child abuse potential inventory', *Journal of Family Violence*, Vol. 25, pp. 215–27

Walker, C. and Davies, J. (2012) 'A cross-cultural validation of the Brief Child Abuse Potential Inventory (BCAP)', *Journal of Family Violence*, Vol. 27, pp. 697–705

The research team includes Dr Noora Ellonen, Dr Sari Lepistö and statistician Mika Helminen, as well as Eija Paavilainen. The work was funded by Etelä-Pohjanmaa and Pirkanmaa Hospital districts, JIK-Joint Municipal Corporation of Social an Ruth Bartlett, University of Southampton d Health Services, Academy of Finland (252106) and University of Tampere, Research Collegium (IASR).

CHAPTER 3

Exploring Risk and Sharing Responsibility in Relation to People with Dementia and GPS

Ruth Bartlett

Ruth Bartlett, University of Southampton

Introduction

What are the risks involved in going outside for people with dementia? And how might Global Position System (GPS) technologies mitigate those risks and help allow for the sharing of responsibility at an individual, familial and community level? Essentially these are the questions that this chapter sets out to explore. Discussion begins by explaining the risks involved in going outside for people with dementia; it then outlines the latest ideas on engagement in community life by people with dementia to show how contact with the outside world can diminish following a diagnosis of dementia. Then, drawing on the latest research on the use of GPS technologies by people with dementia, the chapter weaves an argument for considering the use of such technologies as part of the wider upholding of the rights of people with dementia agenda. It is suggested that, when investigated through a disability lens, GPS technologies have the potential to help build fluid degrees of responsibility at not only an individual level, but also within families and communities.

Getting lost

Getting lost is a common human experience. We can all recall a time when we got lost while out and about: for example, while walking, running, cycling or driving a car in an unfamiliar area. On such occasions we might ask someone for directions, a friend perhaps or someone who knows the area we are in, or the place we are trying to reach. Some people may have a satellite navigation system on their phone or in the car that they use to orientate themselves, although such technology is not 100% reliable, and it maybe the reason why the person got lost in the first place! Nevertheless more and more people are using GPS technology (rather than paper maps) to find their way around. In these kind of circumstances, when a healthy adult (not under the influence of alcohol or drugs) gets lost, one would normally expect that person to take personal responsibility for finding their way again, and the risks to their safety and well-being would be minimal.

The same is not the case for people with dementia, for whom getting lost can be a particularly common and troubling experience. This is because dementia causes changes to higher cortical functioning (such as memory), way-finding abilities and the capacity to process sensory information (such as sounds and visual cues). Thus it is more common for a person with dementia to get lost in familiar surroundings, than someone without this condition. Research suggests that, of the estimated 500,000 people with dementia in the UK who live in their own homes, 40% will get lost at some point and about 5% (25,000) will get lost repeatedly. Indeed works of fiction have represented this aspect of the dementia experience – think, for example, of the book *Elizabeth is Missing* (2014) by Emma Healey and of the film *Still Alice* released in 2014, and directed by Richard Glatzer and Wash Westmoreland; both book and film feature scenes in which a person with dementia becomes disorientated in a familiar place. Getting lost seems to have become part of our cultural perception of this condition.

In real-life situations, when a person with dementia gets lost, the police and/or a rescue team may be called in to help find them. The latest figures on missing persons show that out of a total of 1,271 searches for a missing person in the UK, 194 (15.3%) were for people with dementia – the highest rate for any group except for those who are suicidal/distressed (Perkins and Roberts, 2011). Similarly Dartmoor Rescue Group has said that the majority of their call-outs are for people with dementia who have got lost. Such events are not only distressing for the families involved, but also time-consuming and expensive for the police and rescue teams who conduct the search. In the UK it has been estimated to cost between £1,325 and £2,415 for an average missing persons investigation (Greene and Pakes, 2012). Repeatedly getting lost is a risky situation, then, as outlined below.

Risks involved

One very real risk for someone with dementia when they get lost is that they will die or be seriously injured. Half of all people with dementia who go missing for more than twenty-four hours die or are seriously injured (Koester, 1998). Take, for example, William Lee, a seventy-seven-year-old man with early dementia, who went missing from his home in Hackney on 21 March 2013 during a spate of cold weather. Four days later he was found dead in Barnet, 19km from his home, after he could not remember how to get back. He died of hypothermia (Bartholomew, 2103). Also there was a case recently of Janet McKay, a eighty-eight-year-old women with dementia whose body was discovered eight days after she went missing (Brooks, 2015). Getting lost when you have dementia poses a potential risk to life.

Because of concerns about a person's physical safety, another risk is that the person will be persuaded to stay indoors and not go out at all; for some family carers this is perceived to be the safest option for ensuring the well-being of a person with dementia (Brittain et al., 2010). In addition the Alzheimer's Society has found that people are less likely to go out once they are diagnosed with the condition, partly because of concerns about getting lost (Alzheimer's Society, 2013). Of even greater concern, one only has to browse through online chat webpages, such as www.caring.com, to realise how routinely some family members lock a person with dementia into a room or the house, so that the person cannot get out. People with dementia are thus at risk of home confinement.

Another risk is that the person has to move into a care home. Researchers suggest that repeatedly getting lost doubles a person's risk of admission to expensive long-term care (White et al., 2010). This is likely to be because caregivers need assistance to deal with the situation but cannot get it, and/or because the person is living alone and community services are not available to meet the person's needs. The reasons and circumstances will inevitably be complex and vary across individuals and families. However the bottom line is that, if a person with dementia regularly leaves the house and gets lost, the chances are that long-term care will be posited as the best and only option for them, where opportunities to go out are likely to diminish (although not necessarily).

This is unfortunate as walking outdoors and 'getting out and about' is a common and valued activity for people with dementia – as it is for most people. Moreover evidence suggests that walking outdoors is beneficial for people with dementia; it can engender a sense of self-worth within individuals (Olsson *et al.*, 2013) and help to extend the period of good-quality life for families (Duggan *et al.*, 2008). Given what we also know about the importance of risk-taking for personal happiness, it seems important that the practice of walking outside is maintained and supported, even though it may involve certain risks.

Before moving the discussion on, let us return to the original point, which was that getting lost is a common human experience. But it is a risky one, particularly for people with a neurological condition such as dementia. So how do we address risk and responsibility in this context? If we take risk to mean exposure to the chance of harm, to realise an incremental net benefit – for example, a person might expose themselves to the chance of getting lost for the pleasure of discovering a new area – then someone with dementia is as entitled as anybody else to take risks. However it becomes controversial if someone is exposed to it involuntarily, as can happen when an individual lacks understanding or capacity. Therefore it is important not only to value risk but also to consider how the responsibilities associated with risk-taking might be shared, and it is to this issue we now turn.

Sharing responsibility

The idea of embracing risk and sharing responsibility has been written about by scholars, especially in regard to matters such as insurance. The idea is pertinent whenever a matter involves members of a community sharing a common goal or interest. For example, educating children with a learning disability can be seen as a form of shared responsibility in that parents, educators, administrators and governments all have a role to play (Will, 1986). The sharing of responsibility does not just happen. People may not realise or accept that they have a role to play. Or they may lack the opportunities and resources to do so. Thus scholars have suggested that shared responsibility requires 'adequate opportunity structures' to facilitate it, especially in later life when support may already be diminishing (Kruse and Schmitt, 2015, p. 135). Creating adequate opportunity structures for embracing risk and sharing responsibilities can take many forms. The key is to create opportunities that allow individuals and organisations to demonstrate and fulfil their commitment to a shared goal.

In this section, the idea of shared responsibility is used in relation to people with dementia. It explores how technology might be used to create an opportunity for sharing responsibility and mitigating the risks associated with people with dementia going outside. Specifically the focus is on GPS.

GPS is a satellite-based navigation system that can be used by anyone who needs to keep track of where he or she is, to find his or her way to a specified location, or know what direction and how fast he or she is going. With the exception of locations where it is not possible to obtain a signal, such as subterranean or underwater locations, a GPS system can locate a person wherever they are. More and more individuals and organisations are using GPS to promote safer walking – defined as 'walking outdoors unaccompanied by a caregiver with minimal risk of becoming lost or experiencing anxiety' (Lindsay *et al.*, 2012). Products such as the *EASE* bracelet (which combines GPS with activity monitoring) and *buddi technology* (which can locate the wearer) are being issued to individuals and families affected by dementia by police forces and local authorities. Other technologies such as GPS armbands may also be developed in the future as we discover more about what works for people with dementia.

One can see, then, how technologies such as GPS might be used to help pool the risks and responsibilities associated with people with dementia going outside. Take, for example, the daughter we heard about in Chapter 1, who felt she had no choice but to move her mother into a care home. This is just the kind of situation where GPS technologies could at least be tried before relocation is considered. GPS works because the technology is integrated into the risk-taking practice. Moreover the responsibility is shared between several individuals and organisations. Take, for example, the Alzheimer's Association Safe Return programme. This is a twenty-four-hour nationwide emergency response service in the US for people with dementia who walk. It works when the person with dementia is wearing Safe Return ID jewellery and, if that person becomes lost, the caregiver can call the twenty-four-hour emergency response line to report it. Thus the responsibility becomes integrated with the technology and is shared between the individual, a family member and service provider. Other systems work in very similar ways.

In the UK and elsewhere, police forces and local authorities are beginning to issue GPS technologies for individuals and families affected by dementia in an effort to promote independence and positive risk-taking for people with dementia. Schemes have been set up, for example, by Sussex and Hampshire constabularies.

However the use of GPS with people with dementia is controversial and divides opinion, particularly among clinicians (Robinson *et al.*, 2007). Some regard it as an infringement of a person's civil liberties whereas others consider it an effective means of maintaining a person's safety. Thus the use of GPS raises deep-seated ethical questions about civil liberties, freedom, social rights and responsibilities, perceptions of risk and quality of life, as well as practical questions about the effectiveness of different technologies to obtain GPS information.

Research on the topic of GPS technologies and people with dementia is burgeoning, but it invariably takes a biomedical perspective. Thus the emphasis is on how GPS technology can help to manage clinical problems and reduce 'caregiver burden'. For example, researchers report that GPS systems can be used in dementia care settings to 'manage wandering behaviour' (Kearns *et al.*, 2007) and reassure caregivers (White *et al.*, 2010). As such the emphasis is on improving the life of carers rather than promoting risk-taking for the person with dementia. Indeed evidence of the value of GPS, as part of an integrated approach or shared responsibility to positive risk-taking, is extremely limited.

Another feature of the GPS dementia research is that it tends to take the perspective of family and professional caregivers. The voice of the person with dementia using the system is noticeably absent. For example, one study sought to examine the ethical aspects of using GPS technology for people with dementia by exploring the attitudes of family and professional caregivers towards this technology (Landau *et al.*, 2010). These researchers conducted four focus groups; one comprising experienced group facilitators of the Israel Alzheimer's Society ($n=20$); another included health and social care professionals from a psychogeriatric team ($n=12$); and there were two family caregiver groups ($n=22$ and $n=14$). They found, with one exception, that family caregivers did not have an ethical problem with using GPS if it protected a person from harm; however professionals were 'reluctant to intervene' and recommend GPS on the grounds that it invades a person's right to privacy (Landau *et al.*, 2010, p. 16). Similarly, a small-scale qualitative project by White *et al.* (2010) examined the views of family caregivers about using GPS to locate a person with dementia. For this project, ten carers were interviewed and the researchers found that people 'preferred to use GPS as a back-up to other strategies' (White *et al.*, 2010, p. 152); however professionals reported feeling uncomfortable and ill-equipped to educate individuals and families around appropriate usage (White *et al.*, 2010, p. 157). Other research confirms that attitudinal issues and ethical concerns, as well as a lack of training and information, are the main barriers to professionals prescribing technology that may be needed and desired by individuals living with ill-health in the community.

Recent research has involved people with dementia and found that GPS technologies are used in different ways by different people (McCabe and Innes, 2013). This finding is backed up by a number of small-scale pilot projects undertaken by various organisations, exploring the use of location technologies with people with dementia. For example, Fife Council in Scotland trialled the use of GPS with people with dementia and their carers, and found it enabled the person with dementia to walk independently outdoors and reduced carer stress and anxiety when the person did so (Fife Council, 2011). Similarly the Dementia Friendly Communities Project in rural Scotland evaluated the use of GPS with two families, both of whom found it beneficial as it gave them the 'freedom to roam' (Dementia Friendly Communities, 2014). There is some evidence then that GPS technologies can be helpful for people with dementia and their families.

Clearly we need to know more about the process of sharing responsibility, especially when it involves using GPS technology and people with dementia; not least because the number of people living with dementia grows across the world, and finding solutions to complex situations (such as getting lost) is becoming more and more urgent. However future research needs to investigate the topic through a disability lens, as opposed to a biomedical one. This means looking, first and foremost, at how effective a system is for enabling positive risk-taking, and thus promoting citizenship. Rather than prioritising the needs of carers, the emphasis should be on using the technology to value and enable positive risk-taking.

Conclusion

This chapter has explored the interplay of risks and responsibilities in the context of someone with dementia who goes out on their own. It has outlined the main risks involved for people with dementia, and explained how GPS is being used to help mitigate the risks. It has been suggested that we should think in terms of a shared responsibility, and to see GPS as part of an integrated and collective approach to enable positive risk-taking. Moreover it has been argued that future research investigates the use of GPS through a disability lens. In that way, the needs and rights of people with dementia will take priority, and risk-taking will be valued by all.

References

Alzheimer's Society (2013) *The Hidden Voice of Loneliness*. Avzailable from www.alzheimers.org.uk/site/scripts/download_info.php?fileID=1677 (accessed 27 June 2016)

Bartholomew, E. (2013) 'Disappearing Hackney dementia sufferer's daughter pens songs about his death', *Hackney Gazette*, 23 June

Brittain, K., Corner, L., Robinson, L. and Bond, J. (2010) 'Ageing in place and technologies of place: The lived experience of people with

dementia in changing social, physical and technological environments', *Sociology of Health and Illness*, Vol. 32, No. 2, pp. 272–87. doi:
10.1111/j.1467–9566.2009.01203.x

Brooks, L. (2015) 'Scottish police under fire again after missing woman lead
was missed' (online). Available from URL: https://www.theguardian.com/
uk-news/2015/sep/25/scottish-police-missing-woman (retrieved 27 June
2016)

Dementia Friendly Communities (2014) 'How people with dementia
achieved their dream to roam free and safe in the remote, rural Scottish
Highlands' (online). Available from URL: http://adementiafriendlycom-
munity.com/wp-content/uploads/2015/06/DFC_-GPS-Booklet1.pdf
(accessed 27 June 2016)

Duggan, S., Blackman, T., Martyr, A. and Van Schaik, P. (2008) 'The impact
of early dementia on outdoor life: A "shrinking world" '? *Dementia*, Vol. 7,
No. 2, pp. 191–204; doi: 10.1177/1471301208091158

Fife Council (2011) 'Safer walking for people with dementia' (unpublished).
Details about the project available from URL: http://awards.cosla.gov.
uk/2011/03/cosla-chairs-award-fife-council-safer-walking-for-people-
with-dementia (accessed 27 June 2016)

Greene, K. S. and Pakes, F. (2012) 'Establishing the cost of missing person
investigations'; doi: 10.1093/police/pat036

Kearns, W. D., Msw, L. W., Kearns, W. D., Rosenberg, D., West, L. and Attitudes, S. A. (2007) 'Attitudes and expectations of technologies to manage
wandering behavior in persons with dementia', *Gerontechnology*, Vol. 6, No.
2, pp. 89–101; doi: 10.4017/gt.2007.06.02.004.00

Koester, R. J. (1998) 'The lost Alzheimer's and related disorders subject: New
research and perspectives', *NASAR Proceedings*, Response 98, Chantilly, VA:
National Association of Search and Rescue, pp. 165–81

Kruse, A. and Schmitt, E. (2015) 'Shared responsibility and civic engagement
in very old age', *Research in Human Development*, Vol. 12, pp. 133–48

Landau, R., Auslander, G. K., Werner, S., Shoval, N. and Heinik, J. (2010)
'Families' and professional caregivers' views of using advanced technology
to track people with dementia', *Qualitative Health Research*, Vol. 20, No. 3,
pp. 409–19; doi: 10.1177/1049732309359171

Lindsay, S., Brittain, K., Jackson, D., Ladha, C., Ladha, K. and Olivier,
P. (2012) 'Empathy, participatory design and people with dementia', proceedings of the 2012 ACM Annual Conference on Human
Factors in Computing Systems – SIGCHI '12, pp. 521–30;
doi: 10.1145/2207676.2207749

McCabe, L. and Innes, A. (2013) 'Supporting safe walking for people with
dementia: User participation in the development of new technology',
Gerontechnology, Vol. 12, No. 1, pp. 4–15

Olsson, A., Lampic, C., Skovdahl, K. and Engström, M. (2013) 'Persons with
early-stage dementia reflect on being outdoors: A repeated interview
study', *Aging and Mental Health*, Vol. 17, No. 7, pp. 793–800; doi: 10.1080/1
3607863.2013.801065

Robinson, L., Hutchings, D., Corner, L., Finch, T., Hughes, J., Brittain, K. and

Bond, J. (2007) 'Balancing rights and risks: Conflicting perspectives in the management of wandering in dementia', *Health, Risk and Society*, Vol. 9, No. 4, pp. 389–406; doi: 10.1080/13698570701612774

White, E. B., Montgomery, P. and McShane, R. (2010) 'Electronic tracking for people with dementia who get lost outside the home: A study of the experience of familial carers', *British Journal of Occupational Therapy*, Vol. 73, No. 4, pp. 152–9; doi: 10.4276/030802210X12706313443901

Will, M. C. (1986) 'Educating children with learning problems: A shared responsibility', *Exceptional Children*, Vol. 52, No. 5, pp. 411–15

CHAPTER 4

Shifting Focus: Agency and resilience in a self-management programme for people living with dementia

Elaine Wiersma, Carrie McAiney, Lisa Loiselle, Kathy Hickman and David Harvey

Elaine Wiersma,Lakehead University, Canada; Carrie McAiney,McMaster University, Canada; Lisa Loiselle, University of Waterloo, Canada; Kathy Hickman and David Harvey, Alzheimer Society of Ontario, Canada

Introduction

'That's part of the benefit of going through a course like this. It really helps you work through your feelings about what's happening. It's huge.' [Programme participant]
'You're not just listening to someone talk about it. You're participating and it's making you think. I think that's the biggest thing I've got out of this course is the fact that it makes you think and bring those ideas that have been floating back there forward.' [Programme participant]

The definition of dementia, as a set of conditions characterised by a decline in cognitive abilities that interfere with daily life (Alzheimer Society of Ontario, n.d.), clearly and definitively positions dementia within narratives of decline. While the reality of dementia cannot be ignored, the social construction of dementia within narratives of risk and decline has a clear impact on people with dementia (Baldwin, 2008; Mitchell *et al.*, 2013). The current discourse and attitudes towards people with dementia continue to marginalise them as assumptions are quickly made about their capabilities (Bartlett and O'Connor, 2010; Beard, 2004; Harman and Clare, 2006; Menne *et al.*, 2002). Indeed stigma is a common experience of living with dementia (Burgener *et al.*, 2015). However, with earlier diagnosis, many more people living with dementia are actively advocating, speaking out and staying well longer (Bartlett, 2014a; 2014b; Bartlett and O'Connor, 2010; Camp *et al.*, 2005; Clare, 2002).

Stigma, specifically the assumptions about people's capabilities, results in people with dementia becoming perceived by levels of risk to their own safety and the safety of others (Clarke *et al.*, 2011). Clarke *et al.* argue that judgements and decisions for people living with dementia 'move from a private, internal dialogue about "what is best for me" to an open public/professional debate about "what is best for him"' (Clarke *et al.*, 2011, p. 12). As dementia becomes a defining characteristic of someone's identity after diagnosis (Baldwin, 2008; Mitchell *et al.*, 2013), and actions and behaviours are attributed to dementia, decisions by people living with dementia increasingly become viewed through a lens of risk, with care partners (i.e., family members or friends) and service providers often seeking to keep the person 'safe' (Clarke *et al.*, 2011). These areas of everyday life become contested territories or contested risk (Clarke *et al.*, 2011). For example, everyday activities such as going for a walk, using the stove and going to the shops become constructed within a discourse of risk – that is, the possibility of a negative event occurring (Clarke *et al.*, 2011). While the person with dementia may wish to continue to participate in these activities, others such as family and professional care providers may discourage such 'risk-taking'. As such, the focus in policy, care and interactions is on the deficits of people living with dementia, managing risk and decline (Bailey *et al.*, 2013). These aspects of living with dementia, particularly having dementia becoming a defining characteristic of one's identity, reflect Goffman's (1963) ideas of stigma, whereby negative assumptions become attributed to the person.

What has been less examined however is the concept of resilience. Resilience occurs in the face of adversity, and is a result of a complex and multidimensional interplay between individuals and their communities (Ungar, 2008). An ever-growing body of literature suggests that many people with dementia continue to be resilient, adapt to dementia and other changes, and find purpose and meaning in their lives (Beard, 2004; Harman and Clare, 2006; Harris, 2008; Menne *et al.*, 2002). Harris (2008) has suggested that using a framework of resilience can help illuminate potential risk and vulnerability factors and also highlight the individual strengths, social networks and other community resources for people with dementia. Resilience, then, not only incorporates adaptation on a personal level but also focuses on adaptation on a social and community level. However resilience for people with dementia applied as a concept has been almost completely neglected in the literature (for exceptions see Clarke *et al.*, 2011; Harris, 2008); despite research on adaptations, staying well and the experiences of people with dementia, this has not been positioned within a framework of resilience. Recognising this limitation, a team of researchers set out to develop a self-management programme for people with dementia to enhance adaptation and resilience. Our perspective on self-management is to encourage adaptation, skills, ways of living well, staying positive and understanding how to personally affect change in social networks and community.

This chapter focuses on resilience, along with notions of citizenship and location of expertise, as examined and demonstrated through a participatory action research project to develop a self-management programme for people with dementia. We provide a project overview including information on key concepts that have guided our process such as social citizenship (Bartlett and O'Connor, 2010) and authentic partnerships (Dupuis *et al.*, 2011). We then discuss shifting focus in three main areas:

1. the concept of self-management as a challenge to traditional discourses in dementia, including describing the self-management programme itself and how the programme focuses on the agency of people with dementia;
2. the process of developing the programme using a social citizenship approach;
3. the learning approach of Dialogue Education (Vella, 2008) that is embedded within the programme, and how this approach challenges the location of responsibility and risk expertise.

Project overview

In 2012, funding was received from the Canadian Institutes of Health Research for a multiyear participatory action research project working with people with dementia to develop a self-management programme for people with dementia. The intent of this project was to take existing knowledge about living well with dementia and translate it into a learning programme for people with dementia. Throughout this project, people with dementia and care partners, including family, service providers and facilitators, were engaged in the programme's development. Three people with dementia were part of our research team, and twenty people with dementia were involved in the three advisory hubs as well as more than twenty care partners and service providers. These groups met monthly for one to two years to provide input and feedback on the curriculum development. The programme, called 'Taking Control of Our Lives' and developed by two of the authors (K. Hickman and E. Wiersma), was based on an iterative process of consultation and engagement with the advisory hubs and research team. An environmental scan, consisting of a literature review, review of existing resources and interviews and focus groups with service providers and people with dementia, was conducted at the start of the project.

Agency and self-management

Self-management of chronic disease refers to the ability of individuals to protect and promote health in daily life (Bahrer-Kohler and Krebs-Roubicek, 2009) – in essence, adaptation and resilience in response to living with a chronic condition. Although self-management programmes have been slow to be adopted in dementia care (as an exception, see Martin *et al.*, 2015; Mountain, 2006), research exploring the experiences of people with dementia demonstrates that, despite the changes experienced in dementia, individuals are able to find ways to navigate changes and continue to live well with a diagnosis (Clare, 2002; Harman and Clare, 2006; Harris and Durkin, 2002; Mason *et al.*, 2005; Phinney *et al.*, 2007; Van Dijkhuizen *et al.*, 2006). People with dementia find ways to maintain and preserve a sense of self (Clare, 2002; Harman and Clare, 2006; Harris and Sterin, 1999). Self-management programmes aim to give people the information, tools and support to live well with a chronic condition. In addition, a group environment provides emotional support and the opportunity to learn from peers (Keyes *et al.*, 2014; Ward *et al.*, 2012). Thus, as they are coming to terms with their diagnoses, maintaining a sense of self and continuing to live well, there is a need to ensure that self-management support is integrated into services designed for people with dementia.

While traditional self-management approaches focus on the individual and individual behaviour change, we have understood individuals as situated within a social context, and that agency and structure are always intertwined and shifting and changing (Giddens, 1984). As such, a social citizenship lens enables a greater understanding not only of the agency of the individual, but also of social structures, how these impact an individual, and how individuals can be agents of change within social structures (Bartlett and O'Connor, 2010). As such, while traditional self-management focuses on the individual and self-efficacy, a social citizenship lens enables a greater understanding of the agency of the individual as well as the social structures, how these impact an individual, and how individuals can play a role in shifting and changing these social structures. As such, we see a self-management programme for people with dementia as a potential vehicle not only to provide information and skills for the individual, but also as a potential vehicle to empower the person with dementia to understand and work to shift some of the social structures in his or her context.

From support to 'Taking Control of Our Lives'

The self-management programme is intended to be delivered by Alzheimer Societies in Canada and other organisations sharing similar roles. The eight-week programme involves weekly sessions, each two hours in length, and is designed for people with early dementia. Each topic in the curriculum is approached in a similar manner:

- providing knowledge about the topic;
- sharing personal strategies and/or experiences related to the topic;
- opportunities to try out new ideas;
- identifying strategies that each individual participant wants to try, and developing an action plan to put a strategy in place.

This approach enables participants to examine each topic in relation to their own experiences and to identify, where applicable, strategies they want to use in their lives. In essence participants are building a toolkit of strategies and resources they can draw on as needed.

Participants can choose to attend the programme on their own, or to bring a care partner. If care partners participate, they have their own sessions separate from people with dementia where they cover the same information as the group of individuals with dementia, but with an emphasis on how they can support self-management and resilience for people with dementia.

The curriculum of 'Taking Control of Our Lives'
The programme is divided into four segments: Week 1: Getting started; Weeks 2–4: Foundational skills; Weeks 5–7: Topic-specific skills; and Week 8: Staying well.

Getting started
The first segment of the programme introduces participants to the programme and the way the curriculum will be explored. One of the first discussions is about personal meanings of the term 'self-management' with the goal of developing a common understanding among participants. The 'Getting started' component also includes a discussion of dementia and the changes associated with dementia, enabling participants to explore the changes they have noticed in themselves. It also includes information on memory aids and strategies.

Foundational skills
The group then moves into the development of foundational skills. These skills are essential to building resilience and preparing participants to move on to the 'Topic-specific skills' component. The foundational skills includes modules on: adapting to change; communication; and finding meaning and purpose. The order of each of these three modules is decided by the group.

'Adapting to change' includes exploring the cognitive, physical, emotional and motivational changes that can occur with dementia. Participants explore ways to adapt, in particular through a discussion of resilience and an exploration of what resilience might look like in the face of these changes.

Another foundational skill is 'communication', which includes understanding the changes participants have noticed in their own abilities to communicate, exploring how to have difficult discussions with others, and finding one's own voice by speaking up for one's needs.

The foundation skill of 'finding meaning and purpose' includes exercises aimed at building and maintaining a positive attitude, and finding meaning and purpose within one's own life.

Topic-specific skills

Once again participants determine the order of topics based on personal needs and interests. Three skill areas are explored: building and keeping connections; emotional wellness; and safety, independence and decision-making.

Within the 'building and keeping connections' area, three aspects of connections are explored: meanings of stigma and having conversations about stigma; inclusive spaces, including what constitutes an inclusive space and how to create inclusive spaces; and the importance of connections. The last explores how relationships can change and grow over the dementia journey.

The topic of 'emotional wellness' explores positive and negative emotions experienced after receiving a diagnosis of dementia, issues of grief and loss, and trying out practical ways of managing stress.

The 'safety, independence and decision-making' module has participants examine their own definitions of safety and risk and what is important to them. Participants also explore decision-making within the context of safety and risk.

Staying well

The final week is focused on 'Staying well'. Here participants examine strategies to keep themselves healthy as well as practical tips for working effectively with healthcare providers. Participants reflect on their learnings and experiences during the course of the programme, and discuss ways to maintain positive changes in their lives.

Instead of simply being recipients of support, the programme encourages participants to reflect on their current situations and experiences, celebrate and share the approaches they have used to manage their current circumstances, learn new approaches from peers, and proactively develop plans to build their capacity to live well with dementia.

Shifting focus

From service provision to service development: Engaging people with dementia with a social citizenship lens

This programme was developed using the lens of social citizenship (Bartlett and O'Connor, 2010), which transforms our views of people with dementia from a person to be cared for to a person with agency. It encourages us to think beyond person-centred care where individuals are passive recipients of care to view people as active agents, and is embedded within rights-based discourse (Bartlett and O'Connor, 2010). People with dementia were integral to our work and were equal partners. They had equal voice as contributing members of the team to shape major decisions and actions in the project. We viewed people with dementia as experts in dementia with important insights to contribute to the project.

We supported social citizenship in our process through an Authentic Partnership approach (Dupuis *et al.*, 2011). The Authentic Partnership approach is a framework that guides key stakeholders, including people living with dementia, to work collaboratively, to make shared decisions and to promote social change, equality, empowerment and a sense of enhanced well-being for all. It involves working *with* others, not *for* others (Dupuis *et al.*, 2011). Using an Authentic Partnership approach requires putting away people's assumptions about dementia, valuing the perspectives of all involved, and working interdependently instead of independently. More importantly the Authentic Partnership approach fundamentally recognises that, for a partnership to thrive, everyone's perspectives and contributions must be valued. This is demonstrated in particular by the advisory hubs, which provided input into programme development and also became a source of support and friendship. They provided opportunities for members to feel a sense of accomplishment and of being heard through opportunities to share their experiences, perspectives and opinions on the programme.

There are three guiding principles that need to be in place in order to mobilise Authentic Partnerships: a genuine regards for self and others; synergistic relationships; and a focus on the process. A genuine regard for self and others is a strength-based perspective, which recognises and respects all those involved in the partnership. This includes recognising and upholding human rights, valuing and being valued, knowing others and being known, fostering others' growth and development, and being truly open to others' experience. A synergistic relationship focuses on interdependence and reciprocity, shared mutual learning, building trust and openness to others' perspectives, opinions and ideas. It recognises that we are often stronger when we harness the group's collective abilities and strengths. Focusing on the process allows for new learnings to emerge throughout the process, and not just at the end. When we honour this principle, we view learning as an ongoing, never-ending process. This principle requires openness to 'unlearning' and new learnings, flexibility and patience. Throughout the process of any partnership, opportunities for regular self and group reflection and dialogue are integral to the partnership's success.

The content and objectives of the programme were determined by advisory hub members. There were opportunities for the members to review, try out and provide feedback on parts of the curriculum; they provided important direction in the structure of the programme including the length of the programme and duration of sessions, as well as the role of care partners in the programme. This iterative process was intensive and took a significant amount of time, but was important in operationalising the principles of authentic partnerships. Throughout this iterative process of engaging the advisory hubs in the curriculum development, we focused on understanding the process of engagement and how we could listen better and learn from people with dementia.

From passive learner to learner-knower-teacher and challenging the location of expertise

The self-management curriculum was firmly rooted in Dialogue Education™ (Vella, 2008), an adult education approach reflective of Paulo Freire's critical pedagogy that posits that education is a political act and a form of liberation (Freire, 1968; Kincheloe, 2004). Freire (1968) advocated an approach to education that was dialogical in nature, where learners are decision-makers exploring new ideas and determining how these fit with their experiences rather than being passive recipients of information. Much adult education is delivered using traditional didactic methods with the teacher as authority, yet we know that adults learn best when they are fully immersed in the learning process, when past experiences are the basis for learning, and when learning is meaningful and relevant to the learners' lives (Freire, 1968; Knowles, 1973; Vella, 2008). Within the Dialogue Education™ framework for education, learning is designed to be responsive and accountable to the needs of learners and is facilitated in a respectful and safe way so that learners are both challenged and supported in the process (Global Learning Partners, 2015a). This leads to transformative, lasting learning (Global Learning Partners, 2015a).

The principles and practices used in Dialogue Education™ are based on six key elements of how adults learn (Global Learning Partners, 2015b). These elements include relevance, safety, immediacy, engagement, respect and inclusion. Each of these is carefully attended to in both the design and facilitation of the 'Taking Control of Our Lives' programme, creating a rich learning environment. This learning provides individuals with opportunities for adaptation, while recognising that people will incorporate new ideas that are consistent with their experiences, context and sense of self. Dialogue education is empowering in its approach, recognising the expertise of the learners.

Using this approach, the person with dementia in the programme is positioned in three ways – as learner, knower and teacher. These three roles of learner-knower-teacher effectively challenge the location of expertise, moving it from external to the person with dementia, often rooted in a biomedical model (Baldwin, 2008), stigma and assumptions, to internal, based on the capabilities and strengths of the person with dementia. Positioning people with dementia as learners, knowers and teachers and building on their capabilities and strengths can increase self-confidence and enhance resilience.

Learner: Growth, as a key concept of social citizenship (Bartlett and O'Connor, 2010) underpins our positioning of people with dementia in the 'Taking Control of Our Lives' programme as learners. Learning does not assume a location of expertise external to the person as the capabilities and skills of the learner are important as s/he engages with the material presented (Knowles, 1973; Vella, 2008). Positioning people with dementia as learners challenges traditional tragedy discourses and narratives of decline (Baldwin, 2008; Mitchell et al., 2013) as people with dementia are seen as capable of learning, growing and incorporating new skills into their daily lives.

Knower: A key aspect of adult learning theory and of Dialogue Education™ in particular is that learners are the experts in their own experiences, and that any type of learning should always recognise and build on the experiences and skills of the adult learner (Knowles, 1973; Vella, 2008). Dementia culture is primarily biomedical (Baldwin, 2008; Mitchell *et al.*, 2013), and as such the person with dementia's experiences can be discounted in favour of expert approaches (Baldwin, 2008). Through this project and this programme, we consider people with dementia as knowers of their own experiences. People with dementia have held multiple roles throughout their lives and we acknowledge their expertise in a variety of areas, both in living with dementia and beyond. Thus we relocate the expertise from the biomedical realm to the person with dementia as the knower bringing a variety of expertise to the process. Through this, we challenge social position and implicitly and explicitly acknowledge the experiential expertise of people with dementia as privileged. The curriculum, as such, is built on people's experiences and expertise, and opportunities are presented for people with dementia to share this information.

Teacher: The predominance of a biomedical model suggests that, unless a person's experiences fit within this model, they are discounted (Mitchell *et al.*, 2013). Because of these assumptions, people with dementia are rarely placed in the role as teacher despite the growing body of literature on the importance of peer support (Keyes *et al.*, 2014; Mason *et al.*, 2005) and on people with dementia in leadership and activism roles (Bartlett, 2014a; 2014b; Camp *et al.*, 2005; Lorentzon and Bryan, 2007). In fact much of the literature acknowledges that a key aspect of peer support is the sharing and learning that occur among people with dementia (Mason *et al.*, 2005; Ward *et al.*, 2012). Dialogue Education™ suggests that learners should be engaged with each other, and that learning does not happen from 'teacher' to learner unidirectionally, but when people engage with each other. Within the programme, people with dementia are sharing skills, tips and strategies for living well with others and, when questions arise, the facilitators turn this over to the group for collective problem solving. Understanding that people with dementia have much to teach others is a key underpinning of this programme, consistent with social citizenship (Bartlett and O'Connor, 2010). This repositioning creates agency and builds resilience for people living with dementia.

Conclusions

Throughout this chapter we have demonstrated in practical terms how participatory action research, through the development of a self-management programme for people with dementia, shifts discourses from a biomedical, risk-based discourse to resilience and agency, focusing on how people with dementia continue to live well. The importance not only of developing services to support living well, but also of engaging people with dementia in the development of these services, is an additional way to shift the location of expertise from traditional 'experts' (i.e., service providers) to people with dementia. Using Freire's (1968) underlying values that education is a political act, along with Dialogue Education™ where people are positioned as learners-knowers-teachers, also serves to shift the expertise from traditional experts to people with dementia. Using concepts of agency and resilience through self-management, rights and social citizenship through our process of programme development, and relocation of expertise through Dialogue Education, we have demonstrated how one project – the development of 'Taking Control of Our Lives', a self-management programme for people with dementia – can challenge traditional discourses in dementia.

References

Alzheimer Society Ontario (n.d.). Available from URL: www.alzheimer.ca/en/on/About-dementia/What-is-dementia (accessed 30 October 2015)

Bahrer-Kohler, S. and Krebs-Roubicek, E. (2009) 'Chronic disease and self-management – aspects of cost efficiency and current policies', *Self Management of Chronic Disease: Alzheimer's Disease*, Switzerland: Springer, pp. 1–15

Bailey, C., Clarke, C. L., Gibb, C., Haining, S., Wilkinson, H. and Tiplady, S. (2013) 'Risky and resilient life with dementia: Review of and reflections on the literature', *Health, Risk and Society*, Vol. 15, No. 5, pp. 390–401; doi: 10.1080/13698575.2013.821460

Baldwin, C. and Bradford Dementia Group (2008) 'Narrative(,) citizenship and dementia: The personal and the political', *Journal of Aging Studies*, Vol. 22, pp. 222–8

Bartlett, R. and O'Connor, D. (2010) *Broadening the Dementia Debate: Towards social citizenship*, Bristol: Policy Press

Bartlett, R. L. (2014a) 'The emergent modes of dementia activism', *Ageing and Society*, Vol. 34, No. 4, pp. 623–44

Bartlett, R. L. (2014b) 'Citizenship in action: The lived experiences of citizens with dementia who campaign for social change', *Disability and Society*, Vol. 29, No. 8, pp. 1291–1304

Beard, R. (2004) 'In their voices: Identity preservation and experience of Alzheimer's disease', *Journal of Aging Studies*, Vol. 18, pp. 415–28

Burgener, S. C., Buckwalter, K., Perkhounkova, Y. and Liu, M. F. (2015) 'The effects of perceived stigma on quality of life outcomes in persons with early stage dementia: Longitudinal findings Part 2', *Dementia*, Vol. 14, No. 5, pp. 609–32

Camp, C. J., Skrajner, M. J., and Kelly, M. (2005) 'Early stage dementia client as group leader', *Clinical Gerontologist*, Vol. 28, No. 4, pp. 81–5

Clare, L. (2002) 'We'll fight it as long as we can: Coping with the onset of Alzheimer's disease', *Aging and Mental Health*, Vol. 6, No. 2, pp. 139–48

Clarke, C. L., Wilkinson, H., Keady, J. and Gibb, C. (2011) *Risk Assessment and Management for Living Well with Dementia*. London: Jessica Kingsley

Dupuis, S. L., Gillies, J., Carson, J., Whyte, C., Genoe, R., Loiselle, L. and Sadler, L. (2011) 'Moving beyond patient and client approaches: Mobilizing "authentic partnerships" in dementia care, support and services', *Dementia*, Vol. 11, No. 4, pp. 427–52

Freire, P. (1968) *Pedagogy of the Oppressed*. New York, NY: Bloomsbury Academic

Giddens, A. (1984) *The Constitution of Society*, Cambridge: Polity Press

Global Learning Partners (2015a) 'About dialogue education' (online). Available from URL: www.globallearningpartners.com/about/about-dialogue-education (accessed 20 October 2015)

Global Learning Partners (2015b) 'Six core dialogue education principles in action' (online). Available from URL: www.globallearningpartners.com/downloads/resources/Six_Core_DE_Principles_Revised.pdf (accessed 31 October 2015)

Goffman, E. (1963) *Stigma: Notes on the management of spoiled identity*, New York, NY: Simon and Schuster

Harman, G. and Clare, L. (2006) 'Illness representations and lived experience in early stage dementia', *Qualitative Health Research*, Vol. 16, No. 4, pp. 484–502

Harris, P. and Durkin, C. (2002) 'Building resilience through coping and adapting', in Harris, P. (ed.) (2002) *The Person with Alzheimer's Disease: Pathways to understanding the experience*, Baltimore: The Johns Hopkins University Press, pp. 165–84

Harris, P. B. (2008) 'Another wrinkle in the debate about successful aging: The undervalued concept of resilience and the lived experience of dementia', *International Journal of Aging and Human Development*, Vol. 67, No. 1, pp. 43–61

Harris, P. B. and Sterin, G. J. (1999) 'Insider's perspective: Defining and preserving the self of dementia', *Journal of Mental Health and Aging*, Vol. 5, No. 3, pp. 241–56

Keyes, S. E., Clarke, C. L., Wilkinson, H., Alexjuk, E. J., Wilcockson, J., Robinson, L., Reynolds, J., McClelland, S., Corner, L. and Cattan, M. (2014) '

"We're all thrown in the same boat ...": A qualitative analysis of peer support in dementia care', *Dementia*; doi: 10.1177/1471301214529575

Kincheloe, J. L. (2004) *Critical Pedagogy Primer*, New York, NY: Peter Lang

Knowles, M. (1973) *The Adult Learner: A neglected species*, Houston, TX: Gulf

Lorentzon, M. and Bryan, K. (2007) 'Respect for the person with dementia:
Fostering greater user involvement in service planning', *Quality in Ageing*,
Vol. 8, No. 1, pp. 23–9

Martin, F., Turner, A., Wallace, L. M., Stanley, D., Jesuthasan, J. and Bradbury,
N. (2015) 'Qualitative evaluation of a self-management intervention for
people in early stage of dementia', *Dementia*, Vol. 14, No. 4, pp. 418–35

Mason, E., Clare, L. and Pistrang, N. (2005)' Processes and experiences of
mutual support in professionally-led support groups for people with early-
stage dementia', *Dementia*, Vol. 4, No. 1, pp. 87–112

Menne, H., Kinney, J and Morhardt, D. (2002) ' "Trying to continue to do
as much as they can do": Theoretical insights regarding continuity and
meaning in the face of dementia', *Dementia*, Vol. 1, No. 3, pp. 367–82

Mitchell, G. J., Dupuis, S. L. and Kontos, P. C. (2013) 'Dementia discourse:
From imposed suffering to knowing *other-wise*', *Journal of Applied Herme-
neutics*, June, pp. 1–19. Available from URL: jah.journalhosting.ucalgary.
ca/jah/index.php/jah/article/download/41/pdf (accessed 27 June 2016)

Mountain, G. (2006) 'Self-management for people with early dementia: An
exploration of concepts and supporting evidence', *Dementia*, Vol. 5, pp.
429–46

Phinney, A., Chaudhury, H. and O'Connor, D. (2007) 'Doing as much as I
can: Exploring meaningful activity in dementia', *Aging and Mental Health*,
Vol. 11, No. 4, pp. 384–93

Ungar, M. (2008) 'Resilience across cultures', *British Journal of Social Work*,
Vol. 38, No. 2, pp. 218–35

Van Dijkhuizen, M., Clare, L. and Pearce, A. (2006) 'Striving for connection:
Appraisal and coping among women with early-stage Alzheimer's disease',
Dementia, Vol. 5, No. 1, pp. 73–94

Vella, J. (2008) *On Teaching and Learning: Putting the principles and practices
of dialogue education into action*, San Francisco, CA: Jossey-Bass

Ward, R., Howorth, M., Wilkinson, H., Campbell, S. and Keady, J. (2012)
'Supporting the friendships of people with dementia', *Dementia*, Vol. 11,
No. 3, pp. 287–303

We would like to acknowledge the other members of the Self-Management
of Dementia research team for their contributions to the overall project. We
would also like to acknowledge the Knowledge-to-Action grant received from
the Canadian Institutes of Health Research for this project.

CHAPTER 5

Factors Governing the Development of Resilience in Older People with Dementia and Caregivers

Dympna Casey and Kathleen Murphy

Dympna Casey and Kathy Murphy, National University of Ireland Galway

Introduction

Much of the research on resilience in dementia focuses on the factors that promote resilience rather than on detailed interventions used to build resilience. In this chapter the meaning of resilience in the context of dementia care and the factors that promote resilience in older people, people with dementia and caregivers will be explored. To set the context the chapter opens with a brief overview of the factors that impact on people with dementia in communities. The findings across all studies clearly demonstrate that resilience matters and emphasise the importance of social connectedness, positive social networks and good family relationships in building resilience.

Background

It is estimated that one new case of dementia is added every three seconds (Prince *et al.*, 2015) and once diagnosed the median years of survival is 4.6 (women) and 4.1 (men) (Xie *et al.*, 2008). As well as being a personal burden, dementia often leads to isolation and exclusion (World Health Organization, 2012; Cahill *et al.*, 2012). It is clear that participation of people with dementia in family and civic life is diminished by cultures of exclusion and stigmatisation (Hellstrom, 2002; Wilkinson, 2002; Cahill *et al.*, 2012, World Health Organization, 2012). Social exclusion leads to disempowerment, marginalisation and lack of autonomy, which impede the person with dementia's rights as a citizen (Cantley and Bowes, 2004). It is essential that the personhood and citizenship of people with dementia are recognised (Bartlett and O'Connor, 2010; Cahill *et al.*, 2012). Services in the community are often fragmented and there is poor access to early diagnosis as well as a lack of information, intervention and support (Kelly and Moran, 2010). Vernooij-Dassen *et al.* (2005) examined factors that impact on the diagnosis and early intervention in dementia. Their research, which spanned eight European countries, found that delays in diagnosis were due to a number of factors including a lack of knowledge and stigma. Approaches to dementia care at present are powerfully stigmatising (World Health Organization, 2002) and there is wide variation across Europe in strategies to enhance autonomy, inclusion and empowerment of people with dementia. Inclusion is particularly important as many researchers report that people with dementia are often excluded and marginalised, which in turn contributes to people with dementia being seen as incompetent and incapable with a gradual loss of personhood (Froggatt, 1988; Cotrell and Schulz, 1993; High *et al.*, 1994; Keady, 1996; Downs, 1997; Wilkinson, 2002,). Wilkinson (2002) reports that people with dementia are 'a silent and excluded voice' (Wilkinson, 2002, p. 9), often doubly disadvantaged as cognitive impairment coupled with ageing increased exclusion and disadvantage. Many people with dementia therefore face diminishing personhood and disempowerment unnecessarily. In many countries dementia care is underprioritised and neglected, and carers and people with dementia struggle to cope. The current paradigm of healthcare is one of 'therapeutic nihilism' (Pierce *et al.*, 2013) where the absence of cure leads clinicians to conclude that treatment or interventions are futile. This has led to people with dementia being seen as incompetent and without personhood (Keady, 1996) leading to a reduction in their social engagement (Forbes *et al.*, 2011). In addition people with dementia residing in the community are mainly cared for by informal carers. This role impacts on the carer's quality of life and on their ability to engage in social activities (Volicer, 2005) increasing the risk of mental and physical illness for the caregiver

(Schulz and Martire, 2004). Furthermore the burden of caregiving may result in the person with dementia being placed in residential care prematurely (Cahill *et al.*, 2012).

People with dementia however are 'not passive sufferers but active agents engaged in finding ways to live with and manage the effects' of their condition (Clare *et al.*, 2011). Other research confirms this view indicating that people with dementia are able to retain a sense of self, actively participate in interventions and have the capacity to indicate choices regarding their care (Whitlatch *et al.*, 2005, Murphy *et al.*, 2014). Sabat (2001) argues that many people with dementia could continue to participate in society and retain cognitive abilities for longer if an inclusive psychosocial environment was in place. Theories of resilience provide the basis on which inclusive supportive psychosocial environments for people with dementia can be built, focusing as they do on strengthening people's resources in the face of serious challenges and difficulties (Harris, 2008). Building resilience therefore is a strategy that may help foster social inclusion of people with dementia within communities.

Resilience and dementia

Resilience is defined as 'a dynamic process encompassing positive adaptation within the context of major adversity' (Coleman and Ganong, 2002). Resilience building in dementia, as with resilience building in children and adolescents, focuses on strengthening personal attributes and external assets. It concentrates on modifiable intrapersonal skills and protective factors aimed at increasing a person's 'hardiness', i.e. the ability to remain psychologically and physically healthy, or 'resilient', in the face of adversity. The particular benefit of applying resilience theory to interventions in dementia care 'is the emphasis it places on positive adaptation as a realistic possibility for people with dementia' (Bailey *et al.*, 2013, p. 5).

Harris (2010) also perceives resilience theory as a valuable foundation for exploring the factors that increase the possibility of people with dementia living a meaningful life. In her examination of people with early stage dementia, she identifies key factors distinguishing those who were 'doing ok' (i.e. have exhibited resilience) versus those who were not (Harris, 2010). Her analysis concludes that resilience, far from being a quality that is 'fixed' or innate to some people, can actually be 'taught, encouraged and supported' in everyone. Harris (2010) also supports the view that resilience-boosting interventions must adopt a multifaceted approach to the 'promotion and protection of basic adaptive systems', targeting 'individual, family and community levels'. Her resultant list of 'resilience promoting factors' offers constructive guidance for interventions intended to enhance adaptive function of people with dementia. These promoting factors at the individual level include acceptance of changes in self; emphasis on nurturing remaining skills; focus on positives rather than dwelling on losses; and recognition of the multiple pathways in which a person can make a meaningful contribution to family, friends and/or the community. The promoting factors at the level of family and community include: a supportive doctor; connections to some meaningful community organisation and activity; and a supportive positive social living environment that promotes dignity and respect and attainable independence.

Similarly Windle (2012) identifies resilience as a dynamic lifetime process. She identifies a resilience framework that includes individual, community and societal components impacting upon the resilience of older people with dementia and caregivers. Akin to Harris she perceives resilience as a 'multilevel construct' embracing individual and wider environment (Windle, 2011, p. 163) and highlights the importance of resilience-building intervention for people with dementia, which are multifaceted, holistically targeting the person with dementia, community and society. In order to grasp the idea of 'resilience as process' properly, it is vital to consider assets and protective factors both internal and external: for example, family, community and situational contexts (Harris *et al.*, 2008; Janssen *et al.*, 2011; Masten, 2001; Luthar and Cicchetti, 2000). Psychosocial interventions that strengthen resilience by focusing on the personal attributes and external assets of people with dementia show strong potential (Dröes *et al.*, 2004; Gaugler *et al.*, 2007; Martin-Breen and Anderies, 2011; van Dijk *et al.*, 2012).

However most work on resilience building in dementia is theoretical and preliminary: no empirically tested resilience building interventions involving people with dementia, explicitly using resilient theories, have been reported. Indeed most of the research to date has focused on the factors that govern or promote resilience in older people per se as well as older people with dementia

Factors governing the development of resilience in older people
Harris (2008) identifies a number of key factors important both in maintaining resilience (in this context resilience is defined as a person's capacity to bounce back) and in offsetting risks and vulnerabilities for older people. These include: coping strategies (e.g., problem-solving skills); positive attitude/acceptance of changing self; positive self-concept; productivity; a fighting spirit; religious beliefs; social support networks; community supports; strong family relationships; positive role model(s); and an affirming, person-centred environment (Harris, 2008, pp. 51–9).

Focusing on widowhood and loss of a spouse in later life, Bonanno et al. (2001) identify a number of factors that contribute to resilience including worldview, self-improvement, continuity of identity, enduring relationships and individual roles and behaviours. Likewise Moore and Stratton (2003) focus on loss, but in particular on life for men after the loss of a spouse (n=51). They found that many widowers were resilient. Factors that contributed to widower's resilience included an integrated belief and value system; an optimistic and positive personality; and an ability to get social support. They suggest that resilient men had changed three things: themselves; their environment; and their relationships in that they developed new ones. Bennett (2010) also explores resilience in older widowed men (n=60). She conducted secondary data analysis of interviews undertaken in two UK studies of widowhood. Firstly she examined the data using Bonanno et al.'s (2001) conceptualisation of resilience, which consisted of four criteria: participants viewed their life positively; they were at the time actively engaged in living life; they had returned to a life which had meaning and yielded satisfaction; and they were coping. The interview data of participants

who met this criteria and were deemed resilient was then reana-
lysed and examined using Moore and Stratton's (2003) conceptualisation of resilience, which focused on reorganisation, adaptation,
finding positive benefit and compensation. Bennett (2010) found
that resilient males had good relationships, participated in activities and had resumed a life that had meaning and gave them satisfaction. In this qualitative study four types of resilient widowers
were identified: (1) those who were consistently resilient during
widowhood; (2) those who gradually became resilient; (3) those
who became resilient after a major turning point in their widowhood; and (4) those who had experienced both gradual resilience
and resilience following a major turning point. It was found that
personal characteristics were key influential factors in those men
who were consistently resilient, whereas formal and informal social
support was the important influencing factor for those in group
4. Qualitative research conducted by Wiles *et al.* (2013) in New
Zealand, exploring older people's understandings and experiences
of resilience (n=121), also concludes that older people living with
major illness or hardship can be resilient. Their work reinforces the
view of resilience as a contextualised process 'which can be both
individual and environmental' and has 'multi-layered aspects and
influences' (Wiles *et al.*, 2013, p. 423).

Factors governing the development of resilience in people with dementia

There is also little research available regarding the factors that
people with dementia consider important for building their resilience. We therefore undertook a small descriptive qualitative study
to explore what resilience meant for people with dementia and what
they felt were the factors that facilitated or hindered its development. In total six people with mild to moderate dementia living
in the community in Ireland were interviewed using the CORTE
framework (Murphy *et al.*, 2014). All interviews were recorded and
transcribed verbatim and transcripts were analysed for themes
using the constant comparative technique and the resilience framework developed by Windle (2012). Ethical approval was obtained
from the university ethics committee. Most participants were

female (n=40) and 50% were in the 60–69 age group and 50% in the 70–79 age group. Most had 1–3 years' experience of memory loss, only two participants reported second level educating as their highest level of education attained. When resilience was explained to them as 'bouncing back' in the face of their memory loss, most felt they were to some extent resilient:

> PwD: 'I'd say I have a bit of, you know, that (resilience) in me alright. I'd say that I wouldn't be put down very easily.' (WS320069)

> PwD: 'If I'm partially honest, if I'm fully honest – partially I am and partially I'm not.' (010914)

The main sources of resilience were learning from life experiences and hardships and having resilient parental role models and a sense of gratitude or thankfulness in that there was always someone else less fortunate than they were:

> PwD: 'Ah yea, well see we've been lucky enough. We've been able to, to travel the world … great friends over them years … and had a great time … You know, great memories, like, you know. Well, what I remember.' (080414)

> PwD: 'Mom was a social worker through the Blitz in Manchester. And she had to leave home at 14, because her mum had died, and she had to go working, to make money, and then go to England to support her sister … And I always think of what she has gone through, and what she has done, you know … It gives me the strength.' (010914)

> Interviewer: 'Where did you get that spirit from?'

> PwD: 'From … I'd say it was family kind of. Do you know? … I worked in Dublin first of all, I trained there as a nurse … Seventeen when I left home, that's right.'

> Relative carer: 'And there were times you didn't come home for nine months. You know, it's like you were in America.'

> PwD: 'Yeah, nine months, you'd be a year before you get your holidays … the way it went, you know? It never

bothered me, like, you know, I just took it and went with it
and that was it, you know?' (WS3200069)

Factors that facilitate resilience at the community level included
family and friends, being a member of a dementia advocacy group,
religion and having a pet:

Interviewer: 'And how did you manage to go back [to playing cards]? What happened that made you go back?'

PwD: 'My friend made me.'

Interviewer: 'She knew (about the memory problems), and
she made you?'

PwD: 'Yea, yea, yea she was the first person, I lived next door
to her on xxx Road when we came here thirty-six years ago,
and when her children were young I used to often help, and
we are best buddies, best best buddies.'

Interviewer: 'So that support that you got from her was crucial for you to go back and play the games?'

PwD: 'Yeah.' (010914)

PwD: '... well the [name of local dementia advocacy group]
there's no problem because everybody is expected to have,
by going there you're acknowledging, but there's no sort of
embarrassment about it.' (WS320070)

PwD: 'Having a pet, it helps you ... I take her to [name of
the beach] and she knows the nice ones! ... And they go to
her. And the people then will speak to me. And it's called
the 'Dog Romp' you know, so I go down there, I know I'll
see somebody, I don't know them, but I know their dog, and
likewise ... and there is interaction with people that I never
thought ... yea there is interaction with people that know
me, as me, not as what I was ...' (010914)

PwD: 'And we go to mass every morning, as well.'

Interviewer: 'So religion's very, something that's very
important to you?'

PwD: 'It is, yes, oh it is, yea.'

Interviewer: 'And then from what you said earlier, it helps you cope, so that gives you a, a inner, inner strength'?

PwD:' Strength, it does really, it does, it kind of, whenever I'm kind of, if I ever happen to get down, or worried about something. I say Lord, please help me, be in my corner, you know. So it does, the Lord does.' (080414)

A key barrier to resilience at the community level for many revolved around the changed nature of the urban community where they lived, and they commented that this had changed and there was no longer a sense of community:

Interviewer: 'So would you know a lot of the neighbours now, or are there many of them you don't know?'

PwD: 'Yea, well there are still a few that we, kind of, when we got married and came (husband's name) was always here anyway with his mum. But eh, we, we, there are still a few that we're, they're there but there are a lot of the houses rented … And so you wouldn't know those people.' (080414)

Others reported that they had never really engaged in community activities. Most of these participants were single or had recently moved house to a new location:

Interviewer: '… you've moved here only three months ago but maybe if you'd been still in your own place. Do you think that would help, do you think if you'd more connections with the community?'

PwD: 'Well, the, certainly, on that side of the fence, in relation to where I was. They wouldn't say hello, or goodbye.'

Interviewer: 'You didn't know your neighbours that well?'

PwD: 'No. I didn't take the opportunity, anyway.'

Interviewer: 'How long were you there for, were you there quite a while were you?'

PwD: 'Five years.' (040414)

Having self-confidence, a sense of purpose and having a sense of humour and staying active were identified as factors that facilitated resilience at an individual level:

> PwD: 'Well, generally, I do try to have a positive attitude because I know that if I, if I think negatively about something, I'll say, well right, that's going down the wrong road, you know. And I do try to think positive and himself, as I said, is great support. To think positive, you know. So I, I do feel, definitely, thinking positive, yes.' (080414)

> Interviewer: 'Another thing that people say is about sense of humour and how important that is?'

> PwD: 'A good laugh will do you any good, do you great good.' (WS320069)

> PwD: '… I think it is, I think it's important, yeah, I mean you have to have something that's going to interest you from day to day… and in any part of your life, you really need something, but yeah, it is yeah, important for me to have things to do.' (WS320070)

Some participants identified the lack of personal competence and control of their own environment as factors that hindered resilience at an individual level:

> Interviewer: 'What's the most difficult part for you xx?'

> PwD: 'See the thing about work that gets you out.'

> Interviewer: 'And you work, you do something productive?'

> PwD: 'You do, you can.'

> Interviewer: 'And that's the worst part of having … your problems with your memory now, is that you can't do that?'

> PwD: 'I can't do it, no. I, it seems that I can't but I want to. I, I, I, I'm a broken human being, you know.' (040414)

> PwD: 'No, now I used to read a lot, like, and I enjoyed reading but I've given up on the reading. If I could get that back again I'd be very happy.' (WS320069)

Interviewer: '... actively doing something, cooking the dinner ...'

PwD: 'Ah no I'm not able for that any more.'

Interviewer: 'You're not able for that ...'

Relative carer:' ...they [the children] wouldn't expect her. Ah they wouldn't, in fairness, they'd be bringing us out ...' (020914)

This small study contributes to our understanding of resilience from the perspective of people with dementia and reveals that most feel they are resilience, that key individual and community factors – both internal and external assets – were important in building their resilience. People with dementia felt that they had the capacity to be resilient and that building resilience mattered to them. The findings from this work also resonate with the findings identified earlier in relation to the factors that promote resilience in older people as it too emphasises the importance of social connectedness, positive social networks and good family relationships.

Factors governing the development of resilience in caregivers
The increased number of informal dementia caregivers and consequent high levels of stress they experience have led researchers to focus on promoting resilience among caregivers (Harmell *et al.*, 2011).

Gaugler *et al.* (2007) defined resilience as caregivers' ability to manage stress in line with perceptions of burden and care demands, focusing therefore on effect of resilience rather than participants' experiences. They focused on resilience to discover 'how variations in emotional response (burden) to dementia-related care demands influenced key outcomes (transitions in dementia caregiving such as nursing home placement)' (Gaugler *et al.*, 2007, p. 39). They found that participants with higher levels of resilience at baseline (low burden, high care demands) was associated with less frequent institutionalisation of the person with dementia. The factors associated with building resilience and stress resistance were similar to those mentioned earlier for people with dementia, and included the importance of individual, family and community resources.

Unlike prior approaches that simply explored the direct effects of burden and individual care demands, resilience theory facilitated a more diverse approach taking into account the particular care history, self-concept and social support network of individual caregivers. It therefore provides a cohesive model to support the development of person-centred psychosocial interventions (Gaugler *et al.*, 2007, p. 43).

Harmell *et al.* (2011) conducted a review on the psychobiology of dementia caregiving, focusing in particular on three broad resilience factors – personal mastery, self-efficacy and positive coping style – that appeared to have a positive effect on health outcomes for dementia caregivers. These protective factors were found to mitigate the impact of stress on carer health. A more recent systematic review exploring the definitions, methodological approaches and determinant models related to resilience among caregivers of people with dementia was undertaken by Dias *et al.* (2015). Fifteen studies were included in their review. Findings revealed a lack of consistency in the definitions of resilience used across studies, making comparison difficult. They also found that caregivers with high resilience levels had lower rates of depression, better physical health, were in the older age group, had African-American ethnicity and were female. Social support was identified as a moderating factor of resilience, and various types of support appeared to alleviate the physical and mental overload caused by stress. They recommended the need for more research in this area, in particular in exploring the role of resilience on the physical health of carers (Harmell *et al.*, 2011).

Conclusion

Resilience theory demonstrates much promise in the field of dementia-care issues such as stigma, and isolation of people with dementia must be tackled. There are clear methodological difficulties that need to be addressed including exploring how people with dementia understand and perceive resilience, and the adoption of a consistent definition of resilience across studies. Only then can researchers develop meaningful resilience-building interventions with the potential to improve the quality of life of people with dementia.

References

Bailey, C., Clarke, C. L., Gibb, C., Haining, S., Wilkinson, H. and Tiplady, S. (2013) 'Risky and resilient life with dementia: Review of and reflections on the literature', *Health, Risk and Society,* Vol. 15, No. 5, pp. 390–401; doi: 10.1080/13698575.2013.821460

Bartlett, R. and O'Connor, D. (2010) *Broadening the Dementia Debate: Towards social citizenship,* Bristol: Policy Press

Bennett, K. M. (2010) 'How to achieve resilience as an older widower: Turning points or gradual change?', *Ageing and Society,* Vol. 30, pp. 369–82

Bonanno, G. A., Papa, A. and O'Neill, K. (2001) 'Loss and human resilience', *Applied and Preventive Psychology,* Vol. 10, pp. 193–206

Cahill, S., O'Shea, E. and Pierce, M. (2012) *Creating Excellence in Dementia Care: A research review for Ireland's National Dementia Strategy,* Dublin: Department of Health.

Cantley, C. and Bowes, A. (2004) 'Dementia and social inclusion: The way forward', in Innes, A., Archibald, C. and Murphy, C. (eds) (2004) *Dementia and Social Inclusion: Marginalized groups and marginalized areas of dementia research, care and practice,* London: Jessica Kingsley, pp. 255–71

Clare, L., Kinsella, G. J., Logsdon, R., Whitlatch, C. and Zarit, S. H. (2011) 'Building resilience in mild cognitive impairment and early-stage dementia: innovative approaches to intervention and outcome evaluation', in Resnick, B., Gwyther, L. P. and Roberto, K. A. (eds) (2011) *Resilience in Aging: Concepts, Research, and Outcomes.* New York, NY: Springer Science and Business Media, pp. 245–60

Coleman, M. and Ganong, L. (2002) 'Resilience and families', *Family Relations,* Vol. 51, pp. 101–2

Cotrell, V. and Schulz, R. (1993) 'The perspective of the patient with Alzheimer's disease: A neglected dimension of dementia research', *The Gerontologist,* Vol. 33, No. 2, pp. 205–11

Dias, R., Santos, R. L., Barroso de Sousa, M. F., Nogueira, M. M. L., Torres, B., Belfort, T. and Dourado, M. C. N. (2015) 'Resilience of caregivers of people with dementia: A systematic review of biological and psychosocial determinants', *Trends in Psychiatry and Psychotherapy.* Available from URL: http://www.scielo.br/pdf/trends/2015nahead/2237-6089-trends-2014-0032.pdf (accessed 27 June 2016)

Downs, M. (1997) 'The emergence of the person in dementia research', *Ageing and Society,* Vol. 17, No. 5, pp. 597–607

Dröes, R. M., Meiland, F. J. M., Schmitz, M. and van Tilburg, W. (2004) 'Effect of combined support for people with dementia and carers versus regular day care on behaviour and mood of persons with dementia: Results from a multi-centre implementation study', *International Journal of Geriatric Psychiatry,* Vol. 19, No. 7, pp. 673–84. Available at URL: http://onlinelibrary.wiley.com/doi/10.1002/gps.1142/abstract (accessed 27 June 2016)

Forbes, D., Ward-Griffin, C., Kloseck, M., Mendelsohn, M., St-Amant, O., DeForge, R. and Clark, K. (2011) ' "Her world gets smaller and smaller with nothing to look forward to": Dimensions of social inclusion and exclusion among rural dementia care networks', *Online Journal of Rural Nursing and Health Care,* Vol. 11, No. 2, pp. 27–42

Froggatt, A. (1988) 'Self-awareness in early dementia', in Gearing, B., Johnson, M. and Heller, I. (eds) (1988) *Mental Health Problems in Old Age: A Reader,* Chichester: Wiley, pp. 131–6

Gaugler, J. E., Kane, R. L. and Newcomer, R. (2007) 'Resilience and transitions from dementia caregiving', *Journal of Gerontology: Psychological Sciences,* Vol. 62B, No. 1, pp. 38–44

Harmell, A. L., Chattillion, E. A., Roepke, S. K. and Mausbach, B. T. (2011). 'A review of the psychobiology of dementia caregiving: A focus on resilience factors', *Current Psychiatry Reports,* Vol. 13, pp. 219–24

Harris, P. B. (2010) 'Is resilience a key to living a meaningful life with dementia? Factors that contribute to the resilience process in early stage dementia', Paper presented at the 63rd Annual Scientific Meeting of The Gerontological Society of America, 21 November

Harris, P. B. (2008) Another wrinkle in the debate about successful aging: the undervalued concept of resilience and the lived experience of dementia, *Journal of Aging and Human Development,* 67(1), pp.43–61

High, D. M., Whitehouse, P. J., Post, S. G. and Berg, L. (1994) 'Guidelines for addressing ethical and legal issues in Alzheimer disease research: A position paper', *Alzheimer Disease and Associated Disorders,* Vol. 8, Supplement 4, pp. 66–74

Janssen, B. M., van Regenmortel, T. and Abma, T. A. (2011) 'Identifying sources of strength: Resilience from the perspective of older people receiving long-term community care', *European Journal of Ageing,* Vol. 8, pp. 145–56

Keady, J. (1996) 'The experience of dementia: A review of the literature and implications for nursing practice', *Journal of Clinical Nursing,* Vol. 5, pp. 275–88

Kelly, M. and Moran, M. (2010) 'Forget me not: A study of public health nurses and family carers of people with dementia and Alzheimer's disease in Co. Galway' (online). Available from URL: hse.openrepository.com (accessed 27 June 2016)

Luthar, S. S. and Cicchetti, D. (2000) 'The construct of resilience: Implications for interventions and social policies', *Development and Psychopathology,* Vol. 12, No. 4, pp. 857–85

Martinez-Prather, K. and Vandiver, D. M. (2014) 'Sexting among teenagers in the United States: A retrospective analysis of identifying motivating factors, potential targets and the role of a capable guardian', *International Journal of Cyber Criminology,* Vol. 8, No. 1, pp. 21–35

Moore, A. J. and Stratton, D. C. (2003) *Resilient Widowers: Older men adjusting to a new life,* New York, NY: Prometheus

Murphy, K., Jordan, F., Hunter, A., Cooney, A. and Casey, D. (2014) 'Articulating the strategies for maximising the inclusion of people with dementia in qualitative research studies', *Dementia.* Available at URL: http://dem.sagepub.com/content/early/2014/01/07/1471301213512489.long (accessed 4 December 2014)

Pierce, M., Cahill, S. and O'Shea, E. (2013) 'Planning dementia services: New estimates of current and future prevalence rates of dementia for Ireland', *Irish Journal. of Psychological Medicine*, Vol. 30, No. 1, pp. 13–20

Prince, M., Wimo, A., Guerchet, M., Ali, G.-C., Wu, Y.-T. and Prina, M. (2015) *World Alzheimer Report 2015: The Global Impact of Dementia.* London: Alzheimer's Disease International. Available at URL: www.alz.co.uk/research/WorldAlzheimerReport2015.pdf (accessed 27 June 2016)

Sabat S. R, (2001) *The Experience of Alzheimer's Disease: Life Through a Tangled Veil*, Wiley-Blackwell

Schulz, R. and Martire, L. M. (2004) 'Family caregiving of persons with dementia: Prevalence, health effects, and support strategies', *American Journal of Geriatric Psychiatry*, Vol. 12, No. 3, pp. 240–9

Van Dijk, A. M., Van Weert, J. C. and Dröes, R. M. (2012) 'Does theatre as intervention improve the quality of life of people with dementia?', *International Psychogeriatrics*, Vol. 24, No. 3, pp. 367–81. Available from URL: www.ncbi.nlm.nih.gov/pubmed/22040605 (accessed 27 June 2016)

Vernooij-Dassen, M. J. F. J., Moniz-Cook, E. D., Woods, R. T., De Lepeleire, J., Leuschner, A., Zanetti, O., De Rotrou, J., Kenny, G., Faranco, M., Peters, V., Iliffe, S. and the Interdem group (2005) 'Factors affecting timely recognition and diagnosis of dementia across Europe: From awareness to stigma', *International Journal of Geriatric Psychiatry*, Vol. 20, No. 4, pp. 377–86

Volicer, L. (2005) 'Caregiver burden in dementia care: Prevalence and health effects', *Current Psychosis and Therapeutics Reports*, Vol. 3, No. 1, pp. 20–5

Whitlatch, C. J., Judge, K., Zarit, S. H. and Femia, E. (2005) 'Dyadic intervention for family caregiers and care receivers in early stage dementia', *The Gerontologist*, Vol. 46, No. 5, pp. 688–94

Wiles J. L., Wild K., Kerse N., Allen RES (2012) Resilience from the point of view of older people: 'There's still life beyond a funny knee', *Social Science & Medicine* 74 (3) pp 416–424

Wilkinson, H. (2002) 'Including people with dementia in research: Methods and motivations', in Wilkinson, H. (ed.) (2002) *The Perspectives of People with Dementia: Research methods and motivations*, London: Jessica Kingsley, pp. 9–24

Windle, G. (2011) 'What is resilience? A review and concept analysis', *Reviews in Clinical Gerontology*, Vol. 21, No. 2, pp. 152–69; doi: 10/1017/S0959259810000420

Windle, G. (2012) 'The contribution of resilience to healthy ageing', *Perspectives in Public Health*, Vol. 132, No. 4, pp. 159–60

World Health Organization (2002) *Reducing Risks, Promoting Healthy Life*, World Health Report, Geneva: World Health Organization

World Health Organization and Alzheimer's Disease International (2012) *Dementia: A Public Health Priority*, Geneva: World Health Organization

Xie, J., Brayne, C. and Matthews F. E. (2008) 'Survival times in people with dementia: Analysis from population-based cohort study with 14-year follow-up', *BMJ*, Vol. 336, No. 7638, pp. 58–62

CHAPTER 6

Adolescents, Sexuality and Agency: The Internet as a contested space

Ethel Quayle

Ethel Quayle, University of Edinburgh

Introduction

Contextualising young people's experiences within a broader sociocultural and contemporary media landscape highlights both the changing perceptions around adolescent sexual identity, risk and sexualisation and the increasing intersection between on- and offline behaviours. Within this framework it is necessary to understand the very different kinds of concerns, ethics and aesthetics that pertain to different scenarios. This chapter will consider how constructions of childhood may not only impact on how we frame a 'rights discourse' but also influence our understanding of risks, opportunities and resilience. The backdrop to this chapter will be sexuality and agency, and we will use the ability to produce and share sexual texts and images as an illustrative example of this.

Children's rights

Cordero Arce (2012) in his interesting commentary on children's rights notes that the capacity of children to be 'full rights holders and duty bearers' is denied by our arguments concerning their incompetence, irrationality and immaturity. Our current discourse on children's rights is largely framed by the United Nations Convention on the Rights of the Child (UNCRC, 1989) and suggests that the establishment of a different set of rights from the Universal Declaration of Human Rights (UDHR) must have been because children were seen in some ways to be different to adults.

Underpinning our understanding of rights is the assumption of reason, competence or agency, which children by reason of their 'immaturity' are seen as lacking. Instead the UNCRC argues for the rights of protection, provision and participation, each of which is necessarily construed in relation to an adult (Alderson, 2008). Alderson challenges whether the right to participate is really equivalent to the right to make decisions and to have autonomy, especially given the UNCRC's position on participation as 'the right of the child to be heard'. Ennew (2002) is even critical of this right, particularly as it finds expression at international conferences on children's issues where participation might be seen as 'tokenistic' and driven by an adult agenda of management and containment of what children might say.

Goldstein (1977) argues that implicit in being a child are the notions of being dependent, without capacity and at risk, whereas adults are positioned as risk-takers, independent and having the capacity to decide what is best for themselves (although as discussed in other chapters, not all adults are equal, and many adults are seen as lacking capacity, dependent and at risk).

Cordero Arce (2012) goes on to argue that this emphasis on the innocence of children, their lack of understanding and their dependency both infantalises and disempowers them, and ultimately reduces the advancement of their agency and participation. This is seen in part to be a consequence of rights-based issues being argued in the context of child developmental theory, where the child is seen as moving towards a future (rather than present) independence and competence, with developmental psychology acquiring a powerful position in the regulation of modern childhood (Burman, 2008) (who positions developmental psychology as the 'arbiter of normality': p. 300). Developmental models of childhood drive how we conceptualise the child in relation to both risk factors and protective factors within the environment and the neurobiological effect over the life course on the subsequent developmental trajectory (Woolfenden et al., 2015).

Livingstone and Mason (2015) describe a universal belief that multiple complex changes occur during the overall process of development, from 'a child heavily dependent on his or her family to a young person able to live independently' (Livingstone and Mason, 2015, p. 9), and that development, particularly sexual development, is a complex process that varies depending on individual experiences and cultural contexts. This has relevance for children's rights and the recent and still muted arguments about the rights of sexual expression, particularly in relation to the Internet. Livingstone and Mason (2015) acknowledge that it is problematic to claim an 'autonomous maturational process' (Livingstone and Mason, 2015, p. 9) that takes place from birth without reference to cultural, family and peer influences. However they note that the UNCRC (1989) does in fact specify a child's right to freedom of expression, no matter what the medium of choice.

While the best interests of the child is a primary consideration, we come back full circle to the fact that the best interests are inevitably decided upon by an adult and in a way that is consistent with the evolving capacities of the child. These are challenging issues as there are inevitably tensions around protecting children from what they do not need to know and respecting the rights of older children (adolescents) to find out what they want to know in relation to sexuality. Phillis (2011), in the context of US legislation, suggests that laws that regulate adolescent sexuality can be categorised as either protectionist (enacting restrictions and protections designed to compensate for minors' categorical immaturity) or enabling (recognising adult-like capacity and rights in minors as they progress in their overall development) (Phillis, 2011, p. 275). It is argued that one result of this polarisation might ultimately hurt minors as it results in a lack of coordination of different political and social goals of state legislation.

A qualitative study by Ott and Pfeiffer (2009) of twenty-two 11–14 year olds in relation to their views of sexual abstinence identified three groups: 'That's Nasty', Curious and Normative. These differences in ways of thinking about abstinence were considered to relate to both age and development, where children transition from viewing sex as nasty to being curious about sex. These authors viewed this as a time of openness and vulnerability, which may provide an opportune moment for intervention, by way of providing information about healthy sexuality, pregnancy and sexually transmitted diseases.

In many ways we return again to notions of vulnerability, risk and the prioritisation of the rights of adults to protect children. It seems inevitable whether as policymakers, parents or researchers, that there is an ongoing challenge between children's 'autonomy rights' and their implicit vulnerability and right to protection (Ost, 2013). We will briefly return to this in the context of adolescent self-produced sexual images.

The changing nature of childhood

Shanahan's (2007) work considers that there are many 'child-hoods', as childhood is always constituted in time and space and is influenced by social, political and cultural institutions, and that understanding childhood necessitates revealing the experiences of children. Historical constructions of children were argued by Lee (1982) to have followed three paradigms. The pre-industrial concept of children viewed them as properties, in the same way as other goods owned by an individual. The second saw children as being vulnerable and in need of protection, while in the early twentieth century the child was positioned as someone capable of some level of independence from parents and family. Synnott (1983) also deems notions of childhood to be social categories and reflections of the people who constructed them, and Heywood (2001) goes on to develop this argument further in his discussion of four conceptual dichotomies that are central to discussions of childhood. These dichotomies are: depravity/innocence; nature/nurture; independence/dependence; and age/sex. All of these have relevance to this chapter. The child as pure and innocent is central in the ways that we see childhood today (Kitzinger, 1990), and our response to children whose behaviour is seen to conflict with or undermine this through, for example, criminal activity is to exclude them or to treat them as though they are adults (James and Jenks, 1996). Purity and innocence is also associated with dependence and vulnerability with independence marking the end of childhood (Shanahan, 2007). This also links with the nature/nurture debate, where assumptions are made about the nature of childhood and its 'shaping' into the citizenship of adulthood, and the emerging and gendered notions of sexual beings.

Cordero Arce (2012) argues that western societies in particular value children because they are seen as innocent and in need of protection from all of the dangers posed by the adult world that might threaten this very innocence. This inevitably includes media, strangers, child sexuality and what he describes as 'the "child" acting against "childhood" itself' (Cordero Arce, 2012, p. 379). The construction of childhood as referring to all children under the age of eighteen years is, as we have noted above, the outcome of supranational legislation that focused on the rights of the child. Graupner (2005) argues that the implementation of further legislation by the European Commission in 2000 to combat the sexual exploitation of children and child pornography used the same criteria for sexual protection and abuse to a five-year-old child as well as to a seventeen-year-old adolescent and that this has lead to absurd and dangerous consequences, including potentially the criminalisation of sexual activities between consenting adolescents. Paradoxically older adolescents may also be positioned as agentic in relation to sexual activity, such that the problem of sexual harassment of adolescents in the workplace has received little attention (Boles, 2015).

Risk and opportunities

The distinction between the online and offline environments has become somewhat arbitrary, with interconnectedness and interdependence becoming the norm. Children who have grown up with technology-mediated communication appear to make few distinctions between the online and offline worlds. There is convergent research that demonstrates a relationship between online and offline behaviour, and this is clearly seen in the context of risk. Adolescents who take risks online are also likely to do the same offline, and this too is the case in relation to sexual behaviour (Baumgartner *et al.*, 2012). Concerns about why some children take or are exposed to risks online, especially in relation to sexual behaviour, inevitably comes round to consideration of what makes these children vulnerable. Accounts of vulnerability are intertwined with risk as it is apparent that, while many children take risks, not all children are at risk either of sexual exploitation or of harm (Livingstone and Helsper, 2010). A study of 245

Swedish fifteen year olds and 251 eighteen year olds found that more than half of them had both online and offline sexual and romantic experiences, but age and risk behaviour accounted for higher offline sexual behaviour (Sorbring *et al.*, 2014). However only elevated risk-taking accounted for online sexual/romantic behaviour in boys, while for girls younger age, lower body esteem, higher risk and problem behaviour made a significant contribution. These findings themselves present challenges in terms of both gender-related issues and questions of appropriate developmental behaviour.

Stepping outside the developmental debate is difficult as we have a set of expectations that as children get older they need to take more risks in order to gain independence and develop resilience. Sexual risk-taking might be construed as one of the 'problem spaces' described by Oswell (2013). Livingstone and Mason (2015) argue that concerns about overly sexualised behaviour of adolescents, particularly in relation to girls, may be disproportionate and represent middle class fears, which seek to protect largely white, heterosexual children. However there are also concerns that exposure to the pervasive sexualisation of women and girls may have a negative influence of women's aspirations and potentially lead to an overvaluing of appearance and sexual attractiveness. In part this may be driven by exposure, which may be unintentional or intentional, to online pornographic material. There are considerable differences across countries in terms of exposure to online pornography (Livingstone *et al.*, 2011), although across many studies it is not always clear what content is referred to and whether the person came across content accidentally. There seems to be strong evidence that boys are more likely to seek out pornography online and view a wider array of sexual media, including content that might be considered paraphilic (Sabina *et al.*, 2008); however little attention has been paid in most research as to the nature of the media viewed. Accessing pornographic content has also been associated with other forms of victimisation as well as risk-taking behaviours such as substance use (Ybarra and Mitchell, 2005), poorer mental health and more troubled relationships with parents. However it remains unclear in most studies what the direction of the relationship is between pornography exposure and health and social relationships – does pornography exposure result in reduced well-being or does reduced well-being result in pornography use?

The relationship between online risks and opportunities is complex, but the EU Kids Online research demonstrates that the more children use the Internet the more they become digitally skilled and can avail themselves of opportunities that bring benefits. Internet use, along with Internet skills and opportunities, increases exposure to risks, which may also be associated with harm (although this is another contentious issue as harm is often operationalised as being bothered or upset). Their twenty-five-country, pan-European survey of 9–16 year olds clearly indicated that not all risk results in harm and that whether or not a child is distressed or harmed by online experiences very much depends on age, gender and socio-economic status, as well as on their resilience and resources to cope with what happens on the Internet. Socio-economic status and online risk are associated, although it is middle class adolescents, not those from working class backgrounds, who encounter more risks, and this correlation is strong when children without home access are included. This however is not the case across all European countries.

Ybarra *et al.* (2007) identify nine online activities that are 'risky'. These include: posting personal information; sending personal information; making rude or nasty comments to others; harassing or embarrassing someone else; meeting someone online; having unknown people on social networking friends lists; deliberately visiting pornography sites; talking about sex with those known only online; and downloading from file-sharing sites. This work was completed in 2007 and since then much has changed about the Internet and social media use, but these nine online activities provide a reasonable foundation for how we think about online risk-taking. White *et al.* (2015) note that there is very little psychological research about the mechanisms that might contribute to online risk-taking, and few existing models of risk-taking have been applied to the online environment. Their study of 122 adolescents (13–17 years) and 172 young adults (18–24 years) used fuzzy trace theory to examine developmental differences in adolescents' and young adults' online risk-taking. Specifically they assessed whether differential reliance on gist representations (which are based on vague, intuitive knowledge) or verbatim representations (based on specific, factual knowledge) could explain online risk-taking. Their results indicate that the adolescent group demonstrated significantly higher intentions to engage in future risky online behaviour, and past risky online behaviours were positively associated with future intentions for adolescents and negatively associated for adults. Within this sample, more than half admitted to taking online risks similar to those described by Ybarra *et al.* (2007). They disclosed personal information to strangers and made friends with people on social networking sites who they did not already know offline. The gist measures of online risk-taking showed protective properties when related to future intentions to engage in risky online behaviour for both age groups, and the use of increased verbatim reasoning was predictive of increased online risk intentions in adolescents.

Defining resilience

As we have noted, exposure to online risks is unavoidable but it is not inevitable that this will result in harm. Avoiding risk exposure, through for example limiting access, is unlikely to allow children to acquire skills in managing negative experiences. However adolescents deal with such experiences in different ways, some of which are more effective than others (Smahel and Wright, 2014). We tend to think of resilience in terms of coping: approaches that we use in response to stressful situations as a way of avoiding harm. Such strategies might be behavioural, emotional or cognitive and are used to manage the internal and external consequences of stressful situations (Aldwin *et al.*, 2011). Thomsen and Greve (2013) argue that the investigation of the developmental conditions leading to coping in childhood and adolescence has been neglected in the past decades. Vandoninck and d'Haenens (2015) note that children respond in many different ways to online risks, and these ways of coping depend on perceived harm, controllability and complexity of the situation. D'Haenens *et al.* (2013) distinguish three categories of coping with online content or contact: fatalistic/passive or passive coping (hoping that the problem will just go away, or stopping using the Internet for a while); communicative coping (talking to someone about the problem); proactive coping (trying to fix the problem, deleting unwelcome content and online blocking of the sender).

Vandoninck and d'Haenens (2015), using a sample of 2,046 Flemish children aged 10–16, examined how children thought they would respond to being confronted by an array of online risks. Children aged 13–16 were asked about two types of content risks (sexual and shocking images) and four types of contact/conduct risks (online bullying; contact with strangers; sexting; personal data/privacy misuse). Their results suggest that adolescents tended to perceive online coping strategies along two dimensions. These were engagement versus disengagement and technical versus non-technical measures. Younger children were likely to engage in behavioural avoidance strategies that involved a medium level of active engagement, and often involved talking to someone about the problem. Of interest, girls were more likely to respond proactively and communicate with others about the problem.

This study raises interesting issues about avoidant strategies, which were seen as an active form of coping and different to indifference, where the child simply did not recognise the problem as a problem and therefore did not employ any coping strategies at all. Vandoninck and d'Haenens (2015) also conclude that development processes did play a role in children's coping, because in adolescence there is an inevitable shift from parents to peers such that peer interactions through online social media are central and 'staying or going away' is not an option. This moves adolescents to adopt highly engaged coping strategies. All of this points to agency, and the ability of many children to use strategies to cope with online risks effectively.

Sexuality and agency: Sexting as an example

One of the risks identified in Vandoninck and d'Haenen's (2015) study was sexting. Sexting can be understood as the sending or posting of sexually suggestive text messages and images, including nude or semi-nude photographs, via mobiles or over the Internet.

Definitions vary however, and some studies may also refer to the receiving of texts and images, or explore an aspect of image content or sexting behaviour such as forwarding or sharing images (Klettke et al., 2014). In spite of variation in estimates of prevalence, there is increasing consensus of a link between sexting and age, with older children engaging in more sexting. Findings on prevalence by gender are less clear, with some studies reporting similar rates of self-producing and sending sexual images between the genders and others suggesting that either boys are more likely to engage in sexually revealing self-exposures (Jonsson et al., 2014) or that more girls engage in sexting behaviours (Martinez-Prather and Vandiver, 2014). Children who identified as sexual minorities were also more likely to have sexted than those identifying as heterosexuals (Rice et al., 2012).

Research to date has tended to focus primarily on sexting prevalence and participant characteristics, which has led to an absence of young people's voices on the process of self-producing and sending sexual images (Cooper et al., 2016). However there is evidence of an emerging 'normalcy discourse' that perceives consensual sexting as a normal, contemporary form of sexual expression and intimate communication within romantic and sexual relationships. Within this context sexting is also frequently associated with positive expressions of mutual affection, bonding and trust as well as fun, flirting and as 'arousal' in anticipation of physical intimacy with the recipient (Renfrow and Rollo, 2014). However central to this is the evidence that young people may feel pressured into sexting and that, for some girls involved in romantic relationships, consenting to 'unwanted' self-produced sexual images is a type of 'sexual compliance' or an 'undesirable price' they have to pay to maintain a good relationship (Drouin and Tobin, 2014). This has been contested by Lee and Crofts (2015) who argue that, while such scenarios occur, they do not reflect the experiences expressed by the majority of girls, who are more likely to express motivations for sexting which are associated with pleasure or desire. Alongside overt pressure from partners, young people's perceptions of peer norms and attitudes can also influence and drive their sexual behaviours (Ringrose et al., 2013).

Concerns about sexting have tended to focus on the potential for young people to have sexual communication and contact with others including sexual harassment, online grooming, sexual pressures and being made the objects of images. In their typology of sexting based on US case-law, Wolak and Finkelhor (2011) highlight a range of 'aggravated' sexting incidents carried out by adults and youths, with individuals intending to harm, harass or embarrass others through behaviours that include deception, exploitation and abuse. It is nevertheless clear that not all young people who engage in sexting will be subject to negative social, emotional or legal consequences.

Consent

Livingstone and Mason (2015) note that across the literature (and particularly in relation to sexting) the issue of consent is a recurring theme. Recognising a distinction between those young people who willingly seek to make and send sexual images, and those who feel some element of coercion, is important within gender debates. Issues around female sexting are often inextricably linked to broader moral concerns about the sexualisation of girls within popular culture and the pressures they face to live up to gendered sexual ideals (Karian, 2012). There is evidence that some girls may have more negative sexting experiences, with the potential for partner and peer pressure to make and send images, and the need to negotiate the social and cultural double standards of female sexual reputation if their activities are made public. However, in contrast to these concerns, some authors have advocated sexting as an opportunity for females to embrace sexual images as a self-mediated practice of creativity and self-reflection (Hasinoff, 2013).

Conclusion

Throughout this chapter we have repeatedly returned to issues of risk, harm, agency and rights, particularly in relation to online sexual behaviour and consent. There is a significant and growing debate between those who advocate the need for child protection and strategies that decrease the likelihood of being exposed to risk, and others who argue the rights of children to have access to sexual content and to be able to express their sexuality online. Gillespie (2013) suggests that consensual sexting between adolescents is an expression of the adolescent's sexual identity and therefore protected by Articles 8 and 10 of the European Convention on Human Rights. It is difficult to envisage an easy resolution to this sometimes contentious debate. Livingstone and Mason (2015) argue that there needs to be more equal gender dynamics, a greater certainty of young people's understanding and ability to give consent, and a better understanding of unique risk factors before we can really consider the merits of a rights-based argument over that of one about protection. It would be difficult to challenge this viewpoint except to suggest a need to consider Cordero Arce's (2012) argument for a more emancipated stance in relation to the experiences of children driving the children's rights movement, which has a particular resonance in relation to our increasingly technology-mediated world.

References

Alderson, P., (2008) *Young Children's Rights*, London: Jessica Kingsley

Aldwin, C. M., Skinner, E. A., Zimmer-Gembeck, M. J. and Taylor, A. (2011) 'Coping and self-regulation across the lifespan', in Fingerman, K., Berg, C., Antonucci, T. and Smith, J. (eds) (2011) *Handbook of Lifespan Psychology*, Berlin: Springer, pp. 563–89

Baumgartner, S. E., Sumter, S. R., Peter, J. and Valkenburg, P. M. (2012) 'Identifying teens at risk: Developmental pathways of online and offline sexual risk behaviour', *Pediatrics*, Vol. 130, No. 6, E1489

Boles, A. (2015) 'Centering the teenage "siren": Adolescent workers, sexual harassment, and the legal construction of race and gender', *Michigan Journal of Gender and Law*, Vol. 22, No. 1, pp. 1–53

Burman, E. (2008) *Deconstructing Developmental Psychology*, London and New York: Routledge

Cooper, K., Quayle, E., Jonsson, L. and Svedin, C. G. (2016) 'Adolescents and self-taken sexual images: A review of the literature', *Computers in Human Behavior*, Vol. 55, pp. 706–16

Cordero Arce, M. (2012) 'Towards an emancipatory discourse of children's rights', *The International Journal of Children's Rights*, Vol. 20, No. 3, pp. 365–421

d'Haenens, L., Vandoninck, S. and Donoso, V. (2013) *How to Cope and Build Online Resilience?*, London: EU Kids Online Network

Drouin, M. and Tobin, E. (2014) 'Unwanted but consensual sexting among young adults: Relations with attachment and sexual motivations', *Computers in Human Behaviour*, Vol. 31, pp. 412–18

Ennew, J. (2002) 'Outside childhood: Street children's rights', in Franklin, B. (ed.) (2002) *The New Handbook of Children's Rights*. London and New York: Routledge

Gillespie, A. (2013) 'Adolescents, sexting and human rights', *Human Rights Law Review*, Vol. 13, No. 4, pp. 623–43

Goldstein, J. (1977) 'Medical care for the child at risk: On state supervention of parental autonomy', *Yale Law Journal,* Vol. 86, pp. 645–70

Graupner, H. (2005) 'The 17-year-old child', *Journal of Psychology and Human Sexuality,* Vol. 16, Nos 2–3, pp. 7–24

Hasinoff, A. A. (2013) 'Sexting as media production: Rethinking social media and sexuality', *New Media and Society,* pp. 1–17; doi: 10.1177/1461444812459171

Heywood, C. (2001) A *History of Childhood*: London: Polity

James, A. and Jenks, C. (1996) 'Public perceptions of childhood criminality', *The British Journal of Sociology,* Vol. 47, No. 2, pp. 315–31; doi: 10.2307/591729

Jonsson, L. S., Priebe, G., Bladh, M. and Svedin, C. G. (2014) 'Voluntary sexual exposure online among Swedish youth – social background, internet behaviour and psychosocial health', *Computers in Human Behaviour,* Vol. 30, pp. 181–90

Karian, L. (2012) 'Lolita speaks: "Sexting", teenage girls and the law', *Crime Media Culture,* Vol. 8, No. 1, pp. 57–73; doi: 10.1177/1741659011429868

Kitzinger, C. (1990) 'Who are you kidding?: Children, power and the struggle against sexual abuse', in James, A. and Prout, A. (eds) (1990) *Constructing and Reconstructing Childhood,* London: Falmer Press

Klettke, B., Hallford, D. J. and Mellor, D. (2014) 'Sexting prevalence and correlates: A systematic literature review', *Clinical Psychology Review,* Vol. 34, pp. 44–53

Lee, J. A. (1982) 'Three paradigms of childhood', *Canadian Review of Social Anthropology,* Vol. 19, pp. 501–698

Lee, M. and Crofts, T. (2015) 'Gender, pressure, coercion and pleasure: Untangling motivations for sexting between young people', *British Journal of Criminology,* Vol. 55, No. 3, pp. 454–73

Livingstone, S. and Helsper, E. (2010) 'Balancing opportunities and risks in teenagers' use of the internet: The role of online skills and internet self-efficacy', *New Media and Society,* Vol. 12, No. 2, pp. 309–29

Livingstone, S. and Mason, J. (2015) 'Sexual rights and sexual risks among youth online' (online), report commissioned by eNACSO, the European NGO Alliance for Child Safety Online. Available from URL: www.cois.org/uploaded/Documentation/For_Consultants_ and_Supporting_Organisations/Affiliated_Consultants/Spotlight/ Susie_March_-_Review_on_Sexual_rights_and_sexual_risks_among_ online_youth.PDF (accessed 18 December 2015)

Livingstone, S., Haddon, L., Görzig, A. and Ólafsson, K. (2011) *Risks and Safety on the Internet: The perspective of European children. Full findings,* London: EU Kids Online, London School of Economics

Martinez-Prather, K. and Vandiver, D. M. (2014) 'Sexting among teenagers in the United States: A retrospective analysis of identifying motivating factors, potential targets and the role of a capable guardian', *International Journal of Cyber Criminology,* Vol. 8, No. 1, pp. 21–35

Ost, S. (2013) 'Balancing autonomy rights and protection: Children's involvement in a child safety online project', *Children and Society,* Vol. 27, No. 3, pp. 208–19

Oswell, D. (2013) *The Agency of Children: From family to global human rights*, New York, NY: Cambridge University Press

Ott, M. A. and Pfeiffer, E. J. (2009) '"That's nasty" to curiosity: Early adolescent cognitions about sexual abstinence', *Journal of Adolescent Health*, Vol. 44, No. 6, pp. 575–81

Phillis, N. (2011) 'When sixteen ain't so sweet: Rethinking the regulation of adolescent sexuality', *Michigan Journal of Gender and Law*, Vol. 17, No. 2, pp. 271–313

Renfrow, D. G. and Rollo, E. A. (2014) 'Sexting on campus: Minimizing perceived risks and neutralizing behaviours', *Deviant Behaviour,* Vol. 35, No. 11, pp. 903–20; doi: 10.1080/01639625.2014.897122

Rice, E., Rhoades, H., Winetrobe, H., Sanchez, M., Montoya, J., Plant, A., Kordic, T. (2012) 'Sexually explicit cell phone messaging associated with sexual risk among adolescents', *Pediatrics*, vol. 130, No. 4, pp. 667–73; doi: 10.1542/peds.2012–0021

Ringrose, J., Harvey, L., Gill, R. and Livingstone, S. (2013) 'Teen girls, sexual double standards and "sexting": Gendered value in digital image exchange', *Feminist Theory*, Vol. 14, pp. 305–23; doi: 10.1177/1464700113499853

Sabina, C., Wolak, J. and Finkelhor, D. (2008) 'The nature and dynamics of internet pornography exposure for youth', *CyberPsychology & Behavior*, Vol. 11, No. 6, pp. 1–3

Shanahan, S. (2007) 'Lost and found: The sociological ambivalence toward childhood', *Annual Review of Sociology*, Vol. 33, pp. 407–28

Smahel, D. and Wright, F. M. (2014) *The Meaning of Online Problematic Situations for Children: Results of qualitative cross-cultural investigation in nine European countries*, London: EU Kids Online Network

Sorbring, E., Skoog, T. and Bohlin, M. (2014) 'Adolescent girls' and boys' well-being in relation to online and offline sexual and romantic activity', *Cyberpsychology: Journal of Psychosocial Research on Cyberspace,* Vol. 8, No. 1; doi: 10.5817/CP2014–1–7

Synnott, A. (1983) 'Little angels, little devils: A sociology of children', *Canadian Review of Sociology and Anthropology*, Vol. 20, pp. 79–95

Thomsen, T. and Greve, W. (2013) 'Accommodative coping in early adolescence: An investigation of possible developmental components', *Journal of Adolescence*, Vol. 36, No. 5, pp. 971–81

UNCRC (United Nations Convention of the Rights of the Child) (1989) 'Human rights' (online). Available from URL: https://treaties.un.org/Pages/ViewDetails.aspx?src=TREATYandmtdsg_no=IV-11andchapter=4andlang=en (accessed 15 July 2015)

S. Vandoninck and L. d'Haenen (2015) 'Children's online coping strategies: Rethinking coping typologies in a risk-specific approach', *Journal of Adolescence*, Vol. 45, pp. 225–36

White, C., Gummerum, M. and Hanoch, Y. (2015) 'Adolescents' and young adults' online risk taking: The role of gist and verbatim representations', *Risk Analysis*, Vol. 35, No. 8, pp. 1407–22

Wolak, J. and Finkelhor, D. (2011) *Sexting: A Typology*, Durham, NH: Crimes

Against Children Research Centre, University of New Hampshire

Woolfenden, S., Williams, K., Eapen, V., Mensah, F., Hayen, A., Siddiqi, A. and Kemp, L. (2015) 'Developmental vulnerability: Don't investigate without a model in mind', *Child: Care, Health and Development*, Vol. 41, No. 3, pp. 337–45

Ybarra, M. and Mitchell, K. (2005) 'Exposure to internet pornography among children and adolescents: A national survey', *Cyberpsychology and Behavior: The impact of the internet, multimedia and virtual reality on behavior and society*, Vol. 8, No. 5, pp. 473–86

Ybarra, M. L., Mitchell, K. J., Finkelhor, D. and Wolak, J. (2007) 'Internet prevention messages: Targeting the right online behaviors', *Archives of Pediatrics and Adolescent Medicine*, Vol. 161, pp. 138–45

CHAPTER 7

The Role of Robotics in Social Care for Older People in Germany

Barbara Klein

Barbara Klein, Frankfurt University of Applied Sciences, Germany

Introduction

In Germany social care plays a crucial role in care homes and thus funding systems have been adapted in order to increase staffing levels significantly in recent years. A broad range of concepts, methods and activities in social care exist, and many more are being developed. These are based on paradigms such as autonomy and the right of self-determination and they imply biography-oriented approaches focusing on residents' personal assets, competencies and resources. With the availability of technologies such as social robots, new concepts like robot-assisted-therapy or robot-assisted activities arise. In this chapter three different types of robots are introduced: the therapeutic robotic plush seal PARO; the telepresence robot GIRAFF; and a humanoid-like telepresence robot TELENOID. These different kinds of robotic embodiment and associated functionalities might contribute to social interaction, a key element for maintaining or establishing resilience. This chapter looks at a variety of resilience-promoting factors for each robot and analyses its possible potential. As these developments are new and unusual in the context of very vulnerable clients, the MEE-STAR model is introduced as a method to evaluate the sociotechnical arrangements from an ethical perspective. Questions pursued are: What is the possible contribution of these robots to social care? How can these technologies promote resilience? What are possible ethical issues to be considered?

Social care for older people in German care homes

In Germany social care in care homes has been recognised as important for establishing well-being and quality of life for residents. (Germany provides inpatient care mainly in care homes, unlike in the UK where there are different institutional forms: residential care homes where besides basic personal care mainly social care is provided; nursing care homes where residents require continuous treatment care and medical attention provided by nurses.) Funding systems have been adapted in recent years with a consequent increase of staff in social care. This section outlines common principles as well as the social care concepts and methods utilised in care homes.

Facts and figures on the development of social care in Germany
Social care for older people covers a broad range of concepts, methods and activities. In Germany the importance of social care is widely acknowledged. Figure 7.1 gives an overview of the increase of social care from 1999 to 2013.

	1999	2009	2011	2013
Nursing care homes (NCH)	8,859	11,634	12,354	13,030
Residents in NCH	573,211	748,889	786,920	821,647
Staff in NCH	440,940	621,392	661,179	685,447
Social care	14,967	25,577	27,122	28,710
Additional staff in social care according to §87b, SGB XI	-	16,350	24,549	27,864
Total staff in social care	**14,967**	**41,927**	**51,671**	**56,574**
Share of social care in total NCH staff	3.4%	6.7%	7.8%	8.3%

Figure 7.1: Development of Social Care in Care homes from 1999 till 2013 (Statistisches Bundesamt 2001, 2011, 2013, 2015. Own calculations).

In 1994/5 Long-Term Care Insurance was introduced in Germany with first statistics gathered in 1999 (Statistisches Bundesamt, 2001). The field of activities in care homes differentiates between 'nursing and care', 'social care', 'housekeeping services', 'building services', 'administration and management' and 'others'. 'Nursing and care' includes activities in basic personal care and (medical) treatment care. 'Social care' covers a variety of activities: for example, organisation of the move into the care facility; administration (file application for the healthcare insurances, social benefits, allowances, power of attorney, legal supervision); (seasonal) design and decoration of the home environment; psychosocial support of residents and relatives; organisation and carrying out activities with the residents; support of the residents' advisory board; and opening the care facility to the community (Alten- und Pflegezentren des Main-Kinzig-Kreises, 1999). At that time the share of social care was only 3.4% of the total workforce in care homes. In 2008 the First Act concerning the Further Development of Longterm Care came into effect, which introduced additional staff for social care – the so-called everyday companions – for people with dementia. The total figure of employees in social care increased to 42,000 – 6.7% of the workforce in care homes just one year after the introduction of the legislation. The German Federal Statistical Office categorises this workforce into social carers and additional staff in social care according to §87b, SGB XI (everyday companions). Social carers usually have professional backgrounds as social workers, occupational therapists, nursing and many others, and with 25,600 staff comprise 4.1% of the total workforce in 2009. The additional staff (according to §87b, SGB XI), the so-called everyday companions, have mainly other (nursing) care backgrounds or other professional qualifications and their numbers are steadily increasing (Statistisches Bundesamt, 2011; 2013; 2015). In order to work as an everyday companion a qualification to practise in a nursing care home is required as well as an annual training course (minimum sixteen hours) (Richtlinien, 2014).

Since 2015 the Second Act to Strengthen Long-Term Care came into force, and funding was provided to increase the number of additional social care staff to 45,000 employees, who can cater for the social care of all residents. In the very near future approximately 74,000 staff will contribute to well-being and quality of life in social care in German care homes.

Concepts of social care in nursing homes

There are guiding principles for care in care homes. Paradigms and general principles that are acknowledged as essential for good quality of life in care homes are:

- autonomy and right of self-determination – *Lebensweltorientierung* (the life course orientation concept developed by Thiersch (Fred, 2004);
- biography-oriented work focusing on each resident's personal assets, competencies and resources (Kraus and Hegeler, 2011; Klein *et al.*, 2015).

In the field of social care in care homes a huge variety of concepts, methods and tools exist in order to ease life and enable residents to have enjoyable moments even though they are often feeling (very) unwell. Major concepts are:

- **Biography work** is universally accepted as a positive approach in care of older people and is defined as the 'aggregate of research approaches in social sciences. Data basis is the presentation of the life story, life style and life experience from the perspective of the person who has lived this life.' (Just-Kroll, 2008) Usually staff in care homes collect and collate information of the life histories of the residents, their preferences and dislikes in order to consider these in their (social) care activities, especially if residents have communication difficulties.
- The implementation of **milieu therapy** is based on creating environments that provide a relaxed atmosphere and psychosocial integration (Falk, 2011). E.g. care homes decorate public spaces according to the different seasons often involving residents in the preparation. Residents can decorate and furnish their rooms as they wish.
- Specifically in dementia care, a kind of 'mixed' methods approach exists where several concepts might be adapted to the situation of the nursing care home: **ROT Reality oriented training** is an approach that seeks to prompt individuals to remember their immediate surroundings and time (Just-Kroll, 2008; Falk, 2011). Examples include newspaper reading and discussion groups, huge calendars and timetables for activities.

SET Self-preservation therapy aims to stabilise the person's own identity by promoting knowledge of their personal history e.g. through videos and life-books (Falk, 2011). **Validation** is a special form of communication that aims at the affirmation of the person diagnosed with dementia and their perceived reality (Falk, 2011).

- **Music/art/literature/theatre therapy** is in place, but often depending on the interests and skills of social care staff in the nursing care home.
- **Occupational therapy** is provided by healthcare professionals utilising a wide range of methods and tools (Just-Kroll, 2008).

Looking at the survey on the effects of the First Act on Further Development of Long-Term Care results demonstrate an improvement not only in social care but also in therapeutic and other services as Figure 7.2 shows (Bundesministerium für Gesundheit, 2011).

The advent of new technologies has enabled social care to employ these for new therapies and activities. Technology-based activities are recent developments and utilise a whole range of different technological possibilities: for example, game consoles to promote mobility exercises; software and apps to support memory training and brain activities; and social and emotional robots to encourage social interaction. The purpose focuses on factors that are known to contribute to well-being and resilience (Lavretsky, 2014).

New field: Robots in social care

This section introduces robots and new social care activities such as robot-therapy and robot-activities.

Since the early 2000s new kinds of robots have been on the market – social or emotional robots that are able to interact with human beings. In this chapter, three different types of robots are introduced and characterised: the robotic plush seal PARO; the telepresence robot GIRAFF; and the humanoid-like telepresence robot TELENOID.

With the emergence of robots that stimulate interaction, Libin and Libin (2004) introduced the term 'robotic psychology' and 'robo-therapy' at the beginning of this century. Discussion now focuses on the ways in which these robots can contribute to social care.

Social activities and care provisions in care homes 1998 and 2010 (%)			Services and therapeutical services in care homes 1998 and 2010 (%)		
	1998	2010		1998	2010
Joint activities in the nursing care home (discussion groups,arts and crafts, ...)	96	99	Memory / orientation training	81	95
Gymnastics, sport activities	84	98	Continence training	89	95
Support for daily activities (reading aloud, shopping small items, etc.)	92	97	Diets / special diets	91	94
Terminal care	88	95	Chiropodist	1	93
Spiritual support / pastoral company	1	91	Hairdressing	1	93
Cinema show / events / culture in the nursing care home	82	89	Physiotherapy or movement therapy	74	84
Joint activities outside the nursing care home	82	88	Basal stimulation	1	83
Separate day groups with special social care for persons suffering from dementia	1	68	Strength- and balance-training (fall prevention)	1	82
Library	1	64	Validation	1	77
Accompaniment of visiting authorities	64	64	Occupational therapy	87	71
Accompaniment of private activities	50	57	Music or dance therapy (esp. for people suffering from dementia)	1	67
Sepcial offers for only female or only male residents (men´s evening, ladies´ club; hen party, . . .)	1	42	Speech therapy (voice and speech training; training for people with difficulties when swallowing)	21	53
"All-night-café" or similar for persons suffering from dementia	1	28	Massage, baths, infrared or electrotherapy	31	34
Religious services for muslims	1	12	Behavioral training	2	28
Special occupational or social care activities with foreign or migrant residents	1	6	Psychotherapy	2	13

1 not collected in 1998;
2 1998 behavioral training and psychotherapy were collected as one category. 17% of care homes provided this service.

Figure 7.2: Social activities and care provision in care homes (Bundesministerium für Gesundheit, 2011, p. 117 author's translation).

PARO, the robotic plush seal

PARO is a robotic plush seal (Figure 7.3) developed by AIST in Japan for therapeutic purposes and is utilised in many countries

Figure 7.3: Robotic plush seal PARO.

throughout the world. PARO is an artificial intelligence emotional robot in the form of a baby harp seal, which was designed to interact with human beings to elicit an emotional attachment to the robot. PARO is 'equipped with the four primary senses' (Wada and Shibata, 2006). Sensors include touch sensors over the robot's body, an infrared sensor, stereoscopic vision and hearing. Actuators include eyelids, upper body motors, front paw and hind limb motors. These sensors 'recognise' behaviour and trigger emotional states and provide the opportunity for the person to communicate with the PARO and the PARO to return the communication (Wada and Shibata, 2006).

These robotic artefacts develop their 'own character' depending on how they are treated, thus becoming individual in that it is difficult to predict how they will act or react on stimuli such as stroking, talking or singing to them.

PARO was highlighted as the most therapeutic robot in the world in the *Guinness Book of Records* in 2003. Worldwide there is a range of research projects and pilot studies on the possible applications for PARO: for example, for seriously ill children in hospitals (Shibata *et al.*, 2001); children with autism (Roberts *et al.*, 2013); people traumatised by tsunamis (presentation by Shibata in September 2014 in Yokohama); children with severe disabilities (Klein, 2011); people with multiple disabilities (Klein, 2011); people suffering from cancer (Perkins, 2012); and people with vigilant coma

(Klein *et al.*, 2014). These studies are mainly qualitative. Smaller, randomised, controlled trials (Robinson *et al.*, 2013) with forty residents in hospital and a care home in New Zealand and with eighteen residents in care homes in Australia (Moyle *et al.*, 2013) are now followed by a large representative randomised controlled trial with 380 residents aged sixty years and older and by a documented diagnosis of dementia in Australia (Moyle *et al.*, 2015).

At Frankfurt University of Applied Sciences, artefacts such as PARO have been utilised in student's teaching research projects for training future social workers and also in a range of bachelor degree theses.

Since 2005 PARO has been on sale as a commercial product, and around a hundred care homes in Germany now utilise the robotic seal.

Two different telepresence robots: GIRAFF and TELENOID

The concept of telepresence is important to understand the potentials of the two telepresence robots GIRAFF and TELENOID. Telepresence according to Wikipedia 'refers to a set of technologies which allow a person to feel as if they were present, to give the appearance of being present, or to have an effect, via telerobotics, at a place other than their true location' (Wikipedia, n.d.)

Steuer (1992) contrasts the terms 'presence' ('as the sense of being in an (natural) environment') with 'telepresence' ('as the experience of presence in an environment by means of a communication medium', thus a 'mediated perception of an environment') (Steuer, 1993, p. 6). Two central dimensions of telepresence are *vividness* as the 'ability of the technology to produce a sensorially rich mediated environment' and *interactivity*, which is 'the degree to which users of a medium can influence the form or content of the mediated environment' (Steuer, 1993 p. 11).

Schloerb (1995) describes the term 'telepresence' and the related term 'virtual presence' 'that a person is *in some sense* present in an environment that is physically remote from the person in space' (Schloerb, 1995, p. 64). Transmitting voice via telephone, additionally video via e.g. videoconferencing systems or Skype are commonly known and accepted. Additionally telepresence robots allow the transmission of movements. Most popular is moving remotely through a building or tele-operation in surgery. Less known is the transmission of haptics (via haptic interfaces objects can be controlled from somewhere in the world and response haptic sensations) and mimics (Yamazaki *et al.*, 2012a).

Telepresence robot GIRAFF

The telepresence robot GIRAFF is a product of the Swedish company GIRAFF Technologies AB and is developed for healthcare purposes (www.giraffplus.eu; accessed 27 June 2016). The system consists of a movable screen equipped with camera, microphone and a base on wheels connected with a height-adjustable bar. The system is not autonomous. A remote user can operate GIRAFF with a PC via mouse and Internet connection utilising an easy-to-use control interface. Communication is possible via speech and video transmission. Additionally the remote operator can navigate GIRAFF through the room of the people where the system is located.

Figure 7.4 shows the GIRAFF telepresence system and the control surface.

Figure 7.4: Telepresence robot GIRAFF and screenshot of the graphical user interface.

The application fields for telepresence robots are not clearly defined and are still in development with respect to technology and to service development. The telepresence robot GIRAFF was developed in the course of several European projects (ExCITE 2010–13, GIRAFFplus 2012–14, VictoryaHome 2013–14 and TERESA 2013–16) in order to develop user-centred design functionalities for healthcare applications. Moyle *et al.* (2014) undertook a feasibility study with GIRAFF in a nursing care home with people with a diagnosis of dementia. At Frankfurt University of Applied Sciences, GIRAFF was tested in a nursing care home in a student's teaching research project. In the project ERimAlter, funded by the Federal Ministry of Education and Research, possible applications of GIRAFF were explored: for example, the suitability for services on home modification and independent living (Klein *et al.*, 2015).

GIRAFF is a commercial product and mainly sold to universities. Until now no professional application within a care setting has been known.

Telepresence robot TELENOID
The telepresence robot TELENOID, first introduced in 2010, has been and is being developed by Hiroshi Ishiguro's teams at the Advanced Telecommunications Research Institute (ATR) and Osaka University. TELENOID is 'a new type of teleoperated android robots with a minimal human likeness design that can present anybody' (Yamazaki *et al.*, 2012a). It is about 80cm long and weighs 5kg. The body of TELENOID is covered with silicon skin in order to feel 'pleasantly similar to human skin' (Yamazaki *et al.*, 2012a). Similarly to GIRAFF, TELENOID is operated by a remote user with a laptop and an Internet connection. As well as the voice transmission, the remote user's facial expression and lip movements are captured by a face recognition system and transmitted on to the TELENOID robot. Additionally the remote user can control movements of the arms of TELENOID (e.g. for hugging) by pressing defined keys on the keyboard of the laptop. Figure 7.5 shows TELENOID and the user interface.

TELENOID has been utilised in a field trial project in Japan with ten elderly women with a diagnosis of dementia (Yamazaki *et al.*,

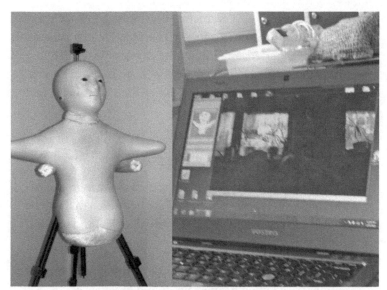

Figure 7.5: Telepresence robot TELENOID and screenshot of the graphical user interface.

2012a; 2012b). In Denmark TELENOID was tested in a two-day trial with two elderly men living in private homes attached to a care facility (Yamazaki *et al.*, 2012a). Another two-day field trial in Japan focused on intergenerational communication between schoolchildren and elderly. At Frankfurt University of Applied Sciences TELENOID was explored in workshops with different user groups and in a one-day field trial with four people diagnosed with dementia as a replication study of Yamazaki *et al.* (2012b).

The development of TELENOID is still an ongoing process and a series of related prototypes are also currently in development.

Robot-assisted social care

With the availability of robots stimulating interaction new therapeutic or activity-oriented methods become possible. Libin and Libin (2004), who introduced the term 'robotic psychology' and 'robotherapy' at the beginning of this century, 'define *robopsychology* as a systematic study of compatibility between people and artificial creatures on many different levels, such as sensory-motor, emotional, cognitive, and social' (Libin and Libin, 2004, p. 1,792) and:

> robotherapy … as a framework of human-robotic crea-
> ture interactions aimed at the reconstruction of a person's
> negative experiences through the development of coping
> strategies, mediated by technical tools, in order to provide
> a platform for building new positive life skills (Libin and
> Libin, 2004, p. 1,793).

Libin and Libin (2004) suggest that there are two goals of psychologically oriented therapy in studying person-robot-interactions:

1. offering a research-justified modification of the robotic crea-
    ture's appearance and behavioural configuration that will be
    suitable for the particular type of psychological and physical
    profile;

2. providing individually tailored, non-pharmaceutical inter-
    ventions based upon people's needs and preferences.

Especially with respect to the second goal, the questions arise about
how far social robots can be utilised in social care in care homes,
what is the difference with respect to other methods and how far
these social robots can contribute to improved well-being?

Figure 7.6 compares the functionalities of the three robots,
their 'communication' and 'emotional' skills as well as other
particularities.

It becomes obvious that PARO is an autonomous robot, compared
to GIRAFF and TELENOID who have to be navigated and operated
by a remote user. However the pedagogical principle of PARO is also
that there is a triangle between the resident, PARO and a facilitator.
The role of the facilitator (social carer) is to stimulate (mediated)
interaction.

GIRAFF and TELENOID are operated by a remote user who can
be a professional care staff member, family, friend or anybody who
has got the connection details. Being similar to a telephone line,
anybody can contact the resident through the GIRAFF or TEL-
ENOID. This opens up a huge potential for possible applications.

The demand for research-based application is important considering that few of the social activities offered in care homes are
evidence based (Stechl et al., 2013).

	PARO	GIRAFF	TELENOID
Movements of robot	Autonomous movements of flippers, eyes, and head. Impression that PARO breathes	Moves through the room according to the handling of the mouse operated by the remote person. (non-autonomous)	Moves head and lips according to the movements of head and lips/mimics of the remote operator. Moves arms through operation of the remote operator (non-autonomous). Impression that TELENOID breathes.
Communication "skills"	Whimpers like a seal, whimpering elucidates whether the robot likes stroking or is hurt by hitting	Voice and video of the operator is transferred (similar to a video conference)	Voice of the remote operator is transferred (comparable to a telephone call)
Emotional "skills"	Babylike features (large head and eyes), people stroke, hug and kiss the robot	–	TELENOID can be hold and hugged
Other features or particularities	Easy to operate	Premises are sufficient bandwidth for the internet connection	TELENOID is still a prototype Embodiment is peculiar, as it reminds of a baby and thus has an impact on the communication of the operator and the recipient

Figure 7.6: Comparison of the functionalities of the three robots.

The underlying questions of whether social robots are suitable for using with vulnerable, frail people and how far they can contribute to resilience for care home residents are central to future research.

Resilience and ethical issues

This section looks at concepts of resilience in order to analyse how far robots can contribute to resilience in adverse life circumstances. Identifying possible therapeutic uses still requires careful consideration of ethical issues. Very often it is questioned whether it is ethical to utilise social robots for vulnerable people. Here the MEE-STAR model for ethical evaluation of sociotechnical arrangements is introduced. Applying the MEESTAR model might be a way to answer questions such as whether trialling or introducing social robots corresponds to ethical requirements.

Resilience-promoting factors in social robots

The concept of resilience might contribute to the discussion and probable decision about whether social robots can be utilised in social care in care homes.

Resilience is a multifaceted concept that has become part of many professional disciplines. It is often explained as 'the ability to bounce back and recover physical and psychological health in the face of adversity' (Van Kessel, 2013, p. 125; Windle, 2011, p. 156).

Van Kessel (2013) reviewed the concept of resilience with respect to the ability of older people to overcome adversity. In her findings **internal factors** (such as caring for self, spirituality, orientation to the future, life experiences with adversity, meaningfulness/purpose of life, caring for others and acceptance) as well as **environmental factors** (such as social support, the ability to access care, social policy, societal responses and availability of resources) play a role in establishing resilience. She then pursues how far 'nurses can enhance outcomes by understanding the role that their own relationship plays as well as social inclusion and connectedness of patients deemed to be experiencing adversity through appropriate referral and linkage' (Van Kessel, 2013, p. 126).

Due to frailty and chronic illnesses the person who has to move into a nursing care home is often faced with several adversities:

decline of their own physical and/or mental and/or psychological state. In general the move can be viewed as a social parting due to loss of physical and mental function. Giving up one's own home and moving into an institution also means reducing belongings and loss of beloved possessions as well as the familiar neighbourhood and friends. Habits and rituals have to be adapted to the requirements, structures and processes of the nursing care home despite the efforts of care homes not to be institutionalising. Figures 7.7 and 7.8 look at internal and external resilience promoting factors from Van Kessel's (2013) review and point out possible contributions for social robots.

Social robots seem to have the potential to contribute to at least some resilience in promoting internal and external factors. However there is still more research needed. Even in the case of TELENOID, which is often perceived as 'creepy' or 'ghost-like' (workshops at Frankfurt University of Applied Sciences), the field trials undertaken by the developers indicate positive effects (Yamazaki *et al.*, 2012a; 2012b). Also the replication study in a German nursing care home indicates that residents and staff consider it possible to explore a robot such as TELENOID in more depth.

Considering the risk and resilience factors mentioned in Chapter 1, experiences with the trialling of the robots in the care facilities showed that 'authoritative voices' play a key role for access in these trials: for example, social workers and nurses suggested residents who they assumed to be very well suited to trial PARO. However relatives and especially legal guardians refused to consent into participation, mainly because of a reluctance towards robots. Misselhorn *et al.* (2013) highlight another ethical dilemma which is changing biographical preferences. If a person with 'an strong intellectual self-identity' has a healthcare directive that excludes the use of emotional robots and this person develops late-stage dementia, moves into a care home and observes emotional robots and then desperately wants to interact with it, a new question arises as to whether 'the self-respect of the person in her former life counts against her affective well-being in the later stages of her life'? (Misselhorn *et al.*, 2013)

Concepts such as 'agency and independence' and 'protection and autonomy' can play a role. However the field trials are scientifically

Internal factors	PARO	GIRAFF	TELENOID
Caring for self/ self-reliance/ independence/self-management/ self-efficacy	Unclear	Unclear; further studies needed	Unclear; further studies needed
Spirituality	Probably not	Remote participation of the resident in (Holy) Masses, spiritual events	Unclear; especially with respect to the embodiment of TELENOID
Orientation to the future/ moving forward with life/ curiosity/ ever seeking/ choosing survival/ will to live/ anticipating on future losses/ generativity	Life-like features of PARO resemble an animal; might contribute to caring behavior similar towards animals	Remote exchange with relatives and friends possible; offers the possibility to carry on with former activities on a remote basis and not having to withdraw due to restricted mobility	In principle similar like GIRAFF; additional possibility to hold TELENOID. Unclear what kind of impact the embodiment has
Life experiences with adversity (frailty, hardship)	Unclear	Unclear; further studies needed	Unclear; further studies needed
Meaningfulness/ purpose in life	Caring for PARO might contribute to sense in own life	Possibility to engage and keep up with former activities in a remote way. More research needed	In principle similar like GIRAFF; additional possibility to hold TELENOID. Unclear what kind of impact the embodiment has
Caring for others/extending self to others, power of giving	Tender exchange by stroking and hugging PARO similar like caring for an animal or baby	Possibility to engage and social exchange with relatives and friends; keeping up friendships	Possibility to engage and social exchange with relatives and friends; keeping up friendships. In principle additional effects as PARO as there is the possibility to hug TELENOID. Effects of embodiment have to be analysed
Acceptance/ acceptance and openness about one's vulnerability/self acceptance	PARO seems to be a mediator in communication; observation that residents reflected their illness (dementia) and its impact	Being able to perform remote activities might contribute to a feeling of self efficacy and thus enabling to accept changed circumstances	TELENOID has in principle the potential to be a mediator and social exchange is possible. Unclear are the effects of the embodiment

Figure 7.7: Internal resilience promoting factors and possible contribution of social robots.

External factors	PARO	GIRAFF	TELENOID
Social Support	Yes, as facilitor for communication	Yes, due to videoconferencing functionality	Yes, due to mimics enhanced communication. Effects of embodiment have to be analyzed.
Supportive relationships of care/ empowering relations with professionals /	PARO enables in some cases a different view on the resident	Unclear; further research needed	Psycho-social potential in therapeutic settings has to be explored; esp. with respect to the embodiment of TELENOID
Social connectedness/ community bonding/ participating in relationship	Has to be explored in future research. Probaly similar to animal related effects	Yes, due to videoconferencing functionality many scenarios are thinkable (e.g. remote visit of theatre etc.; remote participation in municipalities' councils etc.	
Family/friends support/ positive family relationships	PARO can be a mediator e.g. for communication with people suffereing from (severe) dementia	Yes, due to videoconferencing functionality / eventually problematic: monitoring possibilities of GIRAFF	TELENOID could be used as a huggable telephone --> effects have to be explored.
Ability to access care / availability of ressources	In Germany PARO is not acknowledged as a medical device Costs of ca. 5.000 Euro are too high for many nursing care homes. A survey in ERImAlter revealed that most nursing care homes have to find different funding streams.	In Europe telepresence robots are still in a developmental stage and this prevents professional use. Funding will be also an issue and appropriate means and resources have to be found in orde to install such a system.	TELENOID is still a prototype
Social Policy	Validated evidence based effects might contribute to the acknowledgement as a medical device and the inclusion in the catalogue of the European healthcare systems.	Validated evidence based effects might contribute to the acknowledgement as a medical device and the inclusion in the catalogue of the European healthcare systems.	Validated evidence based effects might contribute to the acknowledgement as a medical device and the inclusion in the catalogue of the European healthcare systems.
Social responses/ societal responses	Awareness of the objectives changes social responses which also influence societal responses in the medium term.	Awareness of the objectives changes social responses which also influence societal responses in the medium term.	Awareness of the objectives changes social responses which also influence societal responses in the medium term.

Figure 7.8: External resilience promoting factors and possible contribution of social robots.

limited due to small numbers and lack of control groups. Also the potential of possible applications has not been explored in depth. Here the question arises about whether it is ethical to trial social robots with vulnerable people. Is it deception to the resident if he or she has the impression that the robot is lifelike? What are the potential risks for residents and staff? Do we need guidelines for resilience and ethical promotion of these new technologies?

MEESTAR model to evaluate ethical impact
MEESTAR is a model for the ethical evaluation of sociotechnical arrangements and can be utilised as an analytical instrument 'which guides the process of reflecting on the use of technology' (Manzeschke *et al.*, 2015, p. 13). The MEESTAR cube has seven levels on its z-axis (see Figure 7.9). Some of these levels appear in risk and resilience concepts, however there is variable selectivity.

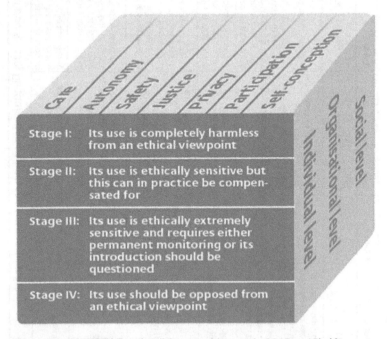

Figure 7.9: MEESTAR cube (Manzeschke *et al.*, 2015, p.15). Key: x-axis – dimensions of ethical evaluation; y-axis – stages of ethical evaluation; z-axis – levels of ethical evaluation.

The seven levels of the cube are associated with key questions (Manzeschke *et al.*, 2015). These are viewed on a social, organisational and individual level. Through a discursive process, decisions can be made about whether the robot's use is completely harmless or should be opposed from an ethical viewpoint.

Figure 7.10 picks up the first question at each of the stages suggested by Manzeschke *et al.* (2015) and attempts tentative answers for the three types of robots.

Social robots not only seem to have factors promoting resilience, but they also appear to have some aspects that could be supported from an ethical perspective. PARO looks suitable as a mediator for social interaction and communication paired with the ability to feed in emotional needs. Whether its lifelikeness is deceit to residents or vulnerable people can probably be judged on a case-to-case basis. Misselhorn *et al.* (2013) discuss these issues in detail from an ethical perspective – work practices in social care are characterised by a pragmatic approach. Residents who react and interact positively to the robot are invited to take part in these group and individual sessions.

The potential of telepresence robots might warrant social inclusion, especially in the case of mobility impairment. However this potential might include inherent risks such as the loss of autonomy and/or privacy as the robot operator may intervene if safety is a prime issue. In general the sociotechnical system has to be considered in order to derive decisions.

Moyle *et al.*'s (2013) feasibility study on GIRAFF shows that people diagnosed with dementia can recognise their relatives on the screen during the video session. Thus the perception of TELENOID has to be investigated in more detail. In one of the encounters a resident mentioned that it looks like 'an unborn baby. It is not ready yet.' In the one-day-trial in Frankfurt residents understood the situation and their reactions to the mediated social carer were comprehensible. It seemed to be more difficult for the social care staff to indulge in the mediated social interaction.

Dimension	Question	PARO	GIRAFF	TELENOID
Care	At which point become social robots problematic for older people because it changes their relationships with themselves and with the world in a way they do not want or which we should not want for them?	If persons interact and accept only PARO and do not communicate with relatives, friends or staff, it might be problematic. However, it is difficult to judge e.g. in case of people in late stage dementia or unresponsive wakefulness.	If direct person-to-person interaction is replaced by merely remote person interaction. However, difficult to judge, there might be cases where it could be the only means for direct interaction.	Similar like GIRAFF: The embodiment of TELENOID might be deceptive and e.g. persons suffering from dementia assume that they are talking to their little child again.
Autonomy	How can people be assisted in their autonomy on the basis of practices oriented consistently around the individual's right to autonomy?	unclear	Residents can be supported in keeping up their social relationships outside and inside the nursing care home. Especially, when residents are very restricted in their mobility or if they are bedridden, GIRAFF could be a supportive instrument.	Similar like GIRAFF: Unclear what the effects of the embodiment are. TELENOID as a "huggable telephone" might be preferred with very close relatives and friends. TELENOID might be a tool to express remote docility.
Safety	How can we encounter the fact that establishing safety can sometimes reduce existing capabilities? In other words, when people begin to rely on technology they may stop taking care of certain things themselves in a productive sense.	Unclear	GIRAFF could be utilized to monitor residents. As there is hardly any experience with that, effects seem to be unclear. Maybe with respect to staff that they might rely on what they perceive through the camera, but the camera might veil the real situation.	Maybe similar to GIRAFF. However, the interface cannot view the remote partner in real. The interface is the android TELENOID. Unclear how communication patterns can develop.
Privacy	How can the privacy of the individual over and above information autonomy be upheld as a moral right when designing age appropriate systems?	Up to now PARO has no monitoring functions. However, these might be different in future. It is imaginable that PARO has a set of sensors that can monitor residents. Then privacy issues have to be taken into account also for people suffering from dementia.	Safety and privacy seem to be contradictory ethical dimensions. Viewing GIRAFF as socio-technical system, adequate measures should be developed in order to avoid ethical conflicts.	It is possible to integrate in TELENOID different kind of health parameter measuring sensors. Aspects of PARO and of GIRAFF are in place and should be considered with respect to the socio-technical system and ethical requirements.
Justice	Who gets access to age appropriate assisting systems?	The costs of PARO are very high. In the U.S. it is acknowledged as a medical device by the FDA. If PARO is approved in Germany, health care insurances might contribute to the costs.	GIRAFF is no medical device and (mobile) telepresence still no standard.	TELENOID is a prototype and applications are still under development.
Participation	What participation is possible for older people? What kind of participation do they wish for?	PARO can be a means to get into interaction with residents suffering from dementia. Cases have been reported where residents started to talk or indicate that they perceive something after a long time they had not interacted with anybody. PARO might provide some emotional attachment, a person might either not be able to offer or is not accepted having that role.	(Mobile) communication offers a variety of application for inclusion of immobile or bedridden patients. It has to be analyzed in how far these new possibilities are accepted by residents.	More research is needed in order to understand the effects of the embodiment and the possibilities for interaction.
Self-conception	How is the question of meaning which tends to pose itself more in old age given space and perspective within socio-technical arrangements?	There is induction training in the use of PARO which entails also meaning of PARO for the resident. Self-conception seems to play a crucial role.	Unclear; more research needed.	Unclear; more research needed.

Figure 7.10: Questions from an ethical perspective and tentative answers (cf. Manzeschke *et al.*, 2015).

Conclusion

The utilisation of these three different kinds of robots is not comparable as they range from a commercial product to a prototype and they serve different purposes. Telepresence might offer new possibilities in stimulating social interaction or even therapeutic intervention for residents in care homes.

A discursive process where stakeholders involved should be included can be a way to reduce risks and stimulate resilience. Bearing this in mind, social robots can open up new ways of interacting in social care for care homes. Nevertheless more research is needed to explore the full potential.

References

Alten- und Pflegezentren des Main-Kinzig-Kreises (ed.) (1999) *Sozialarbeit im Altenpflegeheim: Standards und Perspektiven für die praktische Arbeit*, Kulmbach: Baumann

Bundesministerium für Gesundheit (2011) *Abschlussbericht zur Studie 'Wirkungen des Pflege-Weiterentwicklungsgesetzes'*, Munich: TNS Infratest Sozialforschung. Available from URL: www.bundesgesundheitsministerium.de/fileadmin/dateien/Publikationen/Pflege/Berichte/Abschlussbericht_zur_Studie_Wirkungen_des_Pflege-Weiterentwicklungsgesetzes.pdf (accessed 27 June 2016)

Falk, J. (2011) 'Soziale Arbeit mit demenziell erkrankten Menschen und ihren Angehörigen', in Bieker, R. and Floerecke, P. (eds) (2011) *Träger, Arbeitsfelder und Zielgruppen der Sozialen Arbeit*, Stuttgart: Kohlhammer, pp. 356–72

Fred, K. (2004) 'Demenz und Sozialpädagogik', in Schweppe, C. (ed.) (2004) *Alter und Sozialpädagogik*, Baltmannsweiler: Schneider Verlag.

Just-Kroll, A. (2008) *Biografiearbeit bei demenziell Erkrankten. Ein Schulungskonzept*, Saarbrücken: VDM Verlag Dr Müller

Klein, B. (2011) 'Applications of emotional robotics. First results of teaching research projects at the Fachhochschule Frankfurt', in JDZB (Hg.) (2011) *Human-Robot Interaction from an Intercultural Perspective: Japan and Germany Compared*, Vol. 62, Berlin: Japanese-German Center Berlin, pp. 147–62. Available from URL: www.jdzb.de/veroeffentlichungen/tagungsbaende/band-62 (accessed 27 June 2016)

Klein, B., Kaspar, T. and Zöller, K. (2014) 'Interventions with an emotional robot on patients with unresponsive wakeful syndrome', poster for Conference Universal Village, MIT, Boston, MA, 16–17 June 2014

Klein, B., Kaspar, T. and Schetzkens, R. (2015) 'Models and structural basis of quality of life of people requiring care in nursing homes: Requirements for social work', in Bretländer, B., Köttig, M. and Kunz, T. (eds) (2015) *Diversity and Difference in Social Work: Perspectives on inclusion*, Stuttgart: W. Kohlhammer, pp. 179–91

Kraus, S. and Hegeler, H. (2011) 'Soziale Arbeit in der Geriatrie', in Zippel, C. and Kraus, S. (2011) *Soziale Arbeit für alte Menschen*, Frankfurt am Main: Mabuse-Verlag, pp. 77–93

Lavretsky, H. (2014) *Resilience and Ageing: Research and practice*, Baltimore, MD: Johns Hopkins University Press

Libin, A. V. and Libin, E. V. (2004) 'Person-robot-interactions from the robopsychologists point of view: The robotic psychology and robotic therapy approach', *Proceedings of the IEEE*, Vol. 92, No. 11, pp. 1789–1803

Manzeschke, A., Weber, K., Rother, E. and Fangerau, H. (2015) *Ethical Questions in the Area of Age Appropriate Assisting Systems*, Ludwigsfelde: Druckerei Thiel Gruppe

Misselhorn, C., Pompe, U. and Stapleton, M. (2013) 'Ethical considerations regarding the use of social robots in the fourth age', *GeroPsych*, Vol. 26, No. 2, pp. 121–33

Moyle, W., Beattie, E., Draper, B., Shum, D., Thalib, L., Jones, C., O'Dwyer, S. and Mervin, C. (2015) 'Effect of an interactive therapeutic robotic animal on engagement, mood states, agitation and psychotropic drug use in people with dementia: A cluster-randomised controlled trial protocol', in *BMJ Open*; doi: 10.1136/bmjopen-2015–009097

Moyle, W., Cooke, M., Beattie, E., Jones, C., Klein, B., Cook, G. and Gray, C. (2013) 'Exploring the effect of companion robots on emotional expression in older adults with dementia: A pilot randomized controlled trial', *Journal of Gerontological Nursing*, Vol. 39, No. 5, pp. 46–53

Moyle, W., Jones, C., Cooke, M., O'Dwyer, S., Sung, B. and Drummond, S. (2014) 'Connecting the person with dementia and family: A feasibility study of a telepresence robot', in *BMC Geriatrics*, Vol. 14, p. 7

Perkins, C. (2012) 'Cuddly robots soothe patients in UCI study' (online). Available from URL www.ocregister.com/articles/paro-364274-osgood-patients.html (accessed 27 June 2016)

Richtlinien (2014) 'Richtlinien nach §87b Abs. 3 SGB XI zur Qualifikation und zu den Aufgaben von zusätzlichen Betreuungskräften in stationären Pflegeeinrichtungen (Betreuungskräfte-RI) vom August 2008 in der Fassung vom 29 Dezember 2014' (online). Available from URL: https://www.gkv-spitzenverband.de/media/dokumente/ pflegeversicherung/richtlinien__vereinbarungen__formulare/ rahmenvertraege__richlinien_und_bundesempfehlungen/2014_12_29_ Angepasste_Richtlinien__87b_SGB_XI_final.pdf (accessed 27 June 2016)

Roberts, A. S., Shore, S., Mori, Y., Nazzaro, E. and Maina, J. (2013) 'Playing with a robot: Enhancing social communication and interaction', Poster IMFAR, Randolph, ME: Boston Higashi School

Robinson, H,. Macdonald, B., Kerse, N. and Broadbent, E. (2013) 'The psychosocial effects of a companion robot: A randomized controlled trial', *JAMDA*, Vol. 14, No. 9, pp. 661–7; doi: 10.1016/j.jamda.2013.02.007

Schloerb, D. W. (1995) 'A quantitative measure of telepresence', *Presence*, Vol. 4. No. 1, pp. 64–80

Statistisches Bundesamt (ed.) (2001) *Kurzbericht Pflegestatistik 1999 – Pflege im Rahmen der Pflegeversicherung. Deutschlandergebnisse*, Bonn:

Statistisches Bundesamt
Statistisches Bundesamt (ed.) (2011) *Pflegestatistik 2009. Pflege im Rahmen der Pflegeversicherung. Deutschlandergebnisse*, Wiesbaden: Statistisches Bundesamt
Statistisches Bundesamt (ed.) (2013) *Pflegestatistik 2011. Pflege im Rahmen der Pflegeversicherung. Deutschlandergebnisse*. Wiesbaden: Statistisches Bundesamt
Statistisches Bundesamt (ed.) (2015) *Pflegestatistik 2013. Pflege im Rahmen der Pflegeversicherung. Deutschlandergebnisse*, Wiesbaden: Statistisches Bundesamt
Stechl, E., Knüvener, C., Lämmler, G., Steinhagen-Thiessen, E. and Brasse, G. (2013) *Praxishandbuch Demenz. Erkennen – Verstehen – Behandeln*, Frankfurt am Main: Mabuse-Verlag
Van Kessel, G. (2013) 'The ability of older people to overcome adversity: A review of the resilience concept', *Geriatric Nursing*, Vol. 34, pp. 122–7
Wada, K. and Shibata, T. (2006) 'Robot therapy in a care house – its sociopsychological and physiological effects on the residents', Proceedings 2006 IEEE International Conference on Robotics and Automation, Orlando, FL, 15–19 May 2006, *ICRA*, pp. 3966–71; doi: 10.1109/ROBOT.2006.1642310
Wikipedia (n.d.) 'Telepresence' (online). Available from URL: https://en.wikipedia.org/wiki/Telepresence, accessed 7 November 2015
Windle, G. (2011) 'What is resilience? A review and concept analysis', *Reviews in Clinical Gerontology*, Vol. 21, No. 2, pp. 152–69; doi: 10/1017/S0959259810000420
Yamazaki, R., Nishio, S., Ishiguro, H., Minato, T., Norskov, M., Ishiguro, N., Nishikawa, M. and Fujinami, T. (2012a) *Social Inclusion of Senior Citizens by a Teleoperated Android: Toward inter-generational telecommunity creation*, IEEE/RSJ International Conference on Intelligent Robots and Systems (IROS) Conference, 2012 IEEE International Workshop on Assistance and Service Robotics in a Human Environment
Yamazaki, R., Nishio, S., Ogawa, K. and Ishiguro, H. (2012b) *Teleoperated Androis as an Embodied Communication Medium: A case study with demented elderlies in a care facility*, 21st IEEE International Symposium on Robot and Human Interactive Communication, 9–13 September, Paris, France, pp. 1066–71

Different funding streams and support enabled the work on social robots: BMBF project ERimAlter (emotional and social robots in old age) undertaken by Goethe University and Frankfurt University of Applied Sciences; ATR Advances Telecommunication and Research Institute International and the Intelligent Robotics Laboratory of Prof Dr Hiroshi Ishiguro at Osaka University; Johanna Kirchner Nursing Care Centre of the Johanna Kirchner Foundation; and AWO District Organisation in Frankfurt am Main.

CHAPTER 8

Risk Behaviour among Teenagers: Understanding the social context of teenage pregnancies in two rural schools in the Cape Winelands district, South Africa

Sandra Marais, Ilse Eigelaar-Meets and Caroline Poole

Sandra Marais,formerly South Africa Medical Research Council; Ilse Eigelaar-Meets and Caroline Poole, SOREASO, South Africa

Introduction

Improving the life opportunities of women and young girls has long been a feature of development agendas globally and is now prominent in the Millennium Development Goals. In South Africa substantial efforts have been made to empower women and improve gender equity. The rates of teenage pregnancy have been very high but have declined steadily, yet persist as a source of public and policy concern. Jewkes *et al.* (2009) argue that the key to success in the reduction of teenage pregnancies is an empowering social policy agenda that seeks to work with young people, making them aware of their rights and the risks of sexual intercourse.

Very importantly, as mentioned in Chapter 1, caution should be taken with those who are viewed as vulnerable and at risk so that their individual decision-making and the consequent development of resilience are not compromised: 'It is therefore the intersections between these concepts of risk, rights and resilience that are of critical importance to the well-being of individuals in our societies' (Clarke *et al.*, 2016, p. 4).

Children and youth face multiple risk factors on the path to adulthood – the real challenge is to balance the promotion of autonomy and at the same time render protection.

Background

Literature on the fertility rate in South Africa shows a general agreement that figures have shown a decline among all the major population groups in the country (Anderson, 2003). Analysing 1996
and 2001 census data as well as the 1998 Demographic and Health
Survey, Moultrie and Timæus (2003) show a declining fertility rate
for South Africa since the 1960s. These authors as well as the HSRC
report on fertility (Anderson, 2003) place this marked fertility transition as among the most advanced in Sub-Saharan Africa. More
recent data confirms this slowdown in fertility, with a total number
of 1,199,712 births registered for the year 2006/7 by the South African Department of Home Affairs. This represents a decline of 10%
in registered births (1,346,119) for the same period in 2005/6 (Statistics South Africa, 2008, p. 8). In 2014 this trend continued, with
886,202 registered births reported by Statistics South Africa (Statistics South Africa, 2015)

In spite of this general decline in fertility however, teenage pregnancies (a teenage/adolescent mother is any mother aged nineteen or younger at the time of the birth of her baby; Ehlers, 2003,
p. 15) are still a major concern for government, communities and
researchers. In 2014 some 117,139 young women between the ages
of fifteen and nineteen gave birth – 13.2% of all births in South
Africa (Statistics South Africa, 2015).

According to Anderson (2003, p.14) teenage pregnancies are
more prevalent among Coloured and African girls, particularly
those with little or no education (reference is still made to the
pre-1994 registration of population groups in South Africa, that is
to Coloured, Black, Indian and White because the effects of dis-
crimination are still apparent in the first three population groups).
The use of contraception among young girls and boys is another
concerning aspect that needs mentioning. In her study testing
adolescent mothers' knowledge and perceptions on contraceptives
among teenage mothers in Tswane, South Africa, Ehlers (2003,
p. 19) found that the majority of participants lacked information
on contraceptives. Reasons provided for not using contraceptives
included: that their mothers did not approve; they were ignorant
about contraceptives; they were afraid to go to the clinic because

their mothers might find out; they feared picking up weight and/ or never being able to have children; and their boyfriends opposed their use of contraceptives. For the teenage mothers who indicated they had used contraceptives, the lack of practising and/or maintaining effective contraception resulted in unwanted pregnancies. These findings were confirmed in the study discussed in this chapter.

Risk factors related to teenage pregnancies

The high rate of teenage pregnancies should be approached as an aspect of great concern considering the far-reaching consequences for the young mother and her child. This is especially true for African and Coloured teenage mothers who are among the poorest and most disadvantaged groups in the country. A teenage pregnancy often results in the mother leaving school and terminating her opportunities for personal development, consequently rendering her more vulnerable to poverty, exploitative sexual relationships and violence, as well as resulting in a low self-esteem (Anderson, 2003, p. 14). According to Community Agency for Social Equity (CASE) estimations are that one in every eight (13%) young women has been forced out of the education system as a result of pregnancy. The Department of Health (1999) presents the following statistics on the pregnancy rate for girls within the age group 15–19 years for the different population groups: African 17.8% (13.4% urban; 21.1% non-urban); Coloured 19.3%; White 2.2%; and Asian 4.3% (National Population Unit, 2000, p. 44). The majority of teenage pregnancies are neither planned nor wanted, with the father of the child seldom taking responsibility for the financial, emotional and practical support of the child. Sexual activity at a young age also increases the risk of HIV infection and transmission (Anderson, 2003, p. 14).

Policy responses to teenage pregnancy

The National Department of Health adopted policy guidelines for youth and adolescent health in 2001 and contraception policy guidelines in 2003 (Department of Health, 2001; 2003), both of which state that a range of contraceptives, including emergency contraception and male condoms, should always be in stock at all health facilities. Also information, choice and confidentiality are essential parts of the service. The guidelines emphasise that the healthcare providers should be trained with an emphasis on providing care in a non-judgemental manner (Jewkes *et al.*, 2009). (These two documents have not been updated since 2001 and 2004.)

Furthermore the Department of Education's (2007) guidelines entitled 'Measures for the prevention and management of learner pregnancy' makes it possible for educators to 'request' that learners take a leave of absence from school for up to two years. The 2003 Household Survey statistics indicate that, of all females who had dropped out of school, 13% gave pregnancy as a reason. The relationship between early pregnancy and school disruption is complicated.

To highlight aspects that could be conducive in a social environment resulting in the high-risk behaviour of teenagers, findings from a study conducted in South Africa will be described. The study was commissioned by the Department of Health, Cape Winelands district in 2011, with the specific request to investigate the social environment of teenage sexuality in two secondary schools in a small peri-urban town in the Cape Winelands district. The motivation for this study was the high incidence of teenage pregnancies recorded within these two schools the previous year. Given the great number of risk factors associated with teenage pregnancies, the research team was requested to investigate the circumstances under which these pregnancies took place including an in-depth understanding of the social and home environment of the teenagers in a community that is assumingly conducive to the teenagers' sexual behaviour.

Both qualitative and quantitative methods were employed. The qualitative research methodologies included focus group discussions, in-depth discussions, face-to-face interviews and a stakeholder workshop. Quantitative data was collected by means of a structured questionnaire that was completed by randomly selected learners from both schools.

The primary focus of the structured questionnaire was to test prominence given to high-risk behaviour among the school-going youth. The questionnaire included items within the following themes:

- learner profile and household environment;
- social environment of learner;
- sexual activity and pregnancies;
- substance abuse.

Reporting of research findings on risky behaviours in teenagers

Learner profile and household environment

In total 318 learners participated in our study. The majority of learners from the one school classified themselves as Coloured, with Afrikaans being their home language. In the other school the learners classified themselves as Black, with Xhosa being their home language. The mean age of the learners was fifteen years ranging from thirteen to twenty.

Most of the learners lived in brick houses (such houses are seen in South Africa as a better type of housing than informal, self-built ones) with a mean household size of five people. Less than half of the sample lived with both biological parents with a third living with only the biological mother. On average about 20% of the learners did not live with any biological parent. The greatest majority stated they lived with at least one other sibling with other family members also present in the households such as grandmothers, uncles/aunts, cousins and stepfathers.

Forty-four percent of learners indicated that there was one working person in the household and a further 22% said there were two working people in the household. The greatest majority of learners (78%) reported that the working members worked as labourers at either the local factory or on farms or both during the season.

The following points were found to be important:

- **The perception of seasonal work as permanent employment.** It became clear that the study population perceived seasonal work as full-time/permanent employment. Season time on the farms did not run concurrently with season time at the factory and thus it was possible for a person to be employed for most months of a year even though it was casual work. Thus although work was available in the area it was characterised by seasonality.

- **The impact of the type of work on the social structure of the learner households.** During qualitative interviews the nature of employment was further explored and from these interviews the impact of the type of work, that is, the physical hard and exhausting nature of the work marked by long hours often worked in shifts, on the social structure of the learner households, was highlighted. The parents of teenagers expressed a concern regarding the time that they have to spend away from home in order to work. They often had to work double shifts and some even had to work night shifts resulting in supervision within the household often lacking and teenagers left to their own devices. The mothers also noted that they were often too tired to even think about what their children were up to and often too tired to engage in any sort of communication with their children. This resulted in dysfunctional relationships between parents and their children, leading to even more vulnerability on the side of the child and often in engagement in high-risk behaviour.

- **The state of learner household structures and the case of the absent fathers.** The data shows the minority of learner households in this town to consist of both biological parents with a large percentage of learners living with their biological mothers only. Although the number of single mother households for the two schools is shown as slightly less than the national average (40%), the low number of children living without their biological father in the house may be of concern. In a report on the state of the South African family, Holborn and Eddy (2011) suggest that 'children growing up without fathers are more likely to experience emotional disturbance and depression'. However the claim of the effects of absent fathers on the risky behaviour of teenagers needs more in-depth research.

Sexual activity and pregnancies

A series of questions were asked to find out if the learners were involved in relationships, the use of contraceptives and their knowledge of contraceptives and sexual matters in general. The mean age when learners indicated they had their first sexual experience was at fifteen years (fourteen years for boys and sixteen years for girls). The vast majority (86%) described the nature of their first sexual encounter as 'by choice/I agreed to have sex'. Of these learners who had already had a sexual experience, the majority (62%) indicated that they were currently sexually active.

Date nights were mentioned as the most probable circumstance for sex to take place (40%), and was closely followed by 'no specific circumstance, it just happens' (37%). Learners indicated that they were most likely to have sex after a few drinks. This indicates that sex is mostly not planned but happens in the heat of the moment.

The majority of learners (62%) who were sexually active indicated that they were in 'a love relationship' at the time of the survey. Sexual activity seems to be part of 'a love relationship' and therefore condoned.

The learners indicating that they did not have a previous sexual relationship gave the following reasons for not engaging in sexual relations: I do not want to (42%), and I am not ready to (37%). Religious convictions (7%) and my parents would not approve (5%) were also given as reasons.

The use of contraceptives as learners indicated seems to be relatively high (50%). Condoms were used in most cases (71%) and the injection for the prevention of pregnancies was used in 24% of the cases. When analysing type of contraception used by gender it is important to note that 60% of sexually active females who indicated to use a contraceptive said they used a male condom. Thus in reality they did not use the contraceptive themselves but depended on the partner to do so. Reasons for not using a contraceptive were, among others: 'I don't want my parents to find out'; 'I don't like using it'; 'Sometimes I just don't have it with me'; 'Clinic staff are difficult to approach'; and 'I don't know what it is.'

Girls were asked whether they had been pregnant before or were pregnant at the moment. A total of twelve girls indicated that they had been pregnant before and a further two indicated that they were pregnant at present. The majority of girls were sixteen years when they fell pregnant.

Mostly negative emotions were experienced by the pregnant girls as well as by the parents after their pregnancies have been confirmed. Most were depressed and shocked and angry. Three of the girls did not tell their parents that they were pregnant. Two of the learners said that they went to the hospital for an abortion.

When the male learners were asked about whether their partners have ever been pregnant, two boys indicated that they each had one child. A further two boys indicated that their partners had lost their babies. When asked how they felt when they found out that their partners were pregnant, both boys noted that they had been shocked. The one young man noted that he was also sad, depressed and angry.

Literature on teenage pregnancies suggests that the source of information on reproductive issues seems to play a role in the subsequent behaviour of teenagers. In general friends (31%), mothers (21%) and Life Orientation Classes in school (20%) seemed to play the biggest role in educating the learners. Fathers, possibly because of their absence in the home, played a minor role (3%).

Alcohol and drug abuse

More than half (53%) of the learners indicated that they drunk alcohol. When asked about the frequency of their drinking 49% of the learners indicated that they drunk once a month. A further 33% indicated that they drunk 2–4 times per month

Drug use among the learners was reported as very low with only 5% (N=16) of learners indicating that they did use some kind of illicit drug. When asked what they used, the substances mentioned included dagga (marijuana), hubbly bubbly (smoking substances through a hookah pipe) and Tik (chrystal methamphetamine). Slightly more learners (14%; n=29) indicated that their partners used drugs.

Learners were also asked about their smoking habits. According to learner responses the majority (77%) did not smoke. Most (58%) of the learners who smoked, got through 1–3 cigarettes a day, while

83% of the learners smoked 1–5 cigarettes a day. The mean was four cigarettes a day. Twice as many male learners smoked cigarettes than female learners.

Discussion

In summary the most important issues can be highlighted as follows.

The importance of early interventions

According to the data the majority of learners reported their first sexual experience while in grade 10 (two years before end-of-school education). In testing the sexual activity of learners in romantic relationships, the data clearly shows those learners in grades 8–10 (usually aged 14–16) had not engaged in sexual behaviour while the majority of learners in grades 11 and 12 (usually aged 16–17) who were in romantic relationships are sexually active. It was thus imperative that any interventions on reproductive health be introduced as early as grade 8.

Poor users of contraceptives

In cases where learners were sexually active, many of them did not use of contraceptives or only did so sometimes. The data further shows a large percentage of female learners reporting to use contraception when in fact they were really depending on their partners to use contraception. Thus, in addition to a number of myths with regards to the impact of contraceptive use by female learners (i.e., that your chances of having children diminishes), it is clear that much more needs to be done to educate learners on issues pertaining to reproduction health specifically with regards to contraception. Literature also suggests that more attention should be paid to issues of gender and sexuality, including the terms and conditions under which teenagers have sex. Furthermore workshops on the consequences of not using contraceptives regularly should be included in programmes on reproductive health.

Perceptions with regards to contraceptive use

From the discussions with girls on contraceptive use it was clear that they primarily relied on their partners to ensure that contraption (condoms) was used during sex. This was confirmed in the survey data where 63% of the girls who confirmed using contraception indicated a condom as the type of contraceptive. These girls were thus totally disempowered and fully dependent on their male partners to ensure contraceptive use. Only 36% indicated that they used the contraceptive injection. This is a worrying fact given that boys, when asked about contraceptive used especially in the case of one night stands although not exclusively, indicated this as the girl's responsibility as 'she knows what she is in for'.

Choice not to visit clinic
This was primarily out of fear that their parents would find out that they were sexually active because someone within the community might see them going to the clinic.

Myths with regards to the health impact of female contraception
Much more needs to be done to do away with myths surrounding female contraception with the majority of girls convinced that it would result in weight increase, which would make them unattractive to the boys, or else that it would have a negative impact on their reproductive system if used for too long or from too early an age. Both of these 'beliefs' were false, but had a great effect on the use of contraceptives by girls.

The role of alcohol use and pregnancies
From the teenage focus group discussions and case studies of teenage mothers and fathers the central role of alcohol as part of social events was clearly voiced. Although teenagers were not said to drink to the state of passing out, it was clear from the way alcohol consumption at these events was described that enough was consumed to result in their judgement and inhibitions being compromised. These occasions were also described as opportunities for sex by the boys, who clearly make use of the lower inhibition levels of girls. Given the state of the boys themselves, the control within the sexual act – specifically with regards to contraceptive use – was highly questionable and risky. All factors added to the likelihood of subsequent teenage pregnancies.

The perception of love and sexual relationships as two separate concepts

Information from interviews with teenage fathers (to be) showed that being committed as a boyfriend did not necessarily imply truthfulness in sexual relations. This stands in contrast to the teenage mothers where they all placed commitment within a love relationship as equal to, or to include, commitment within the sexual relationship, thus being truthful included a truthful sexual relationship. From both the focus group discussions with girls and in-depth interviews with teenager mothers/mothers to be it became clear that the reason why girls chose to have sexual relations with boys/men was based on a romanticised perception about the permanence of the romantic relationship. When asked why girls had sex with their boyfriends the answer was always the same, either to prove their love (thus show their commitment) or as a safeguard for not being cheated on by the boyfriend. For the boys, although love did play a role in their choice to have sex, the reason for sexual relations appeared to be much more a case of a want to have the experience. When talking about romantic commitment boys had a clear distinction between love and sex. The boys associated love with a relationship they had with their girlfriend with whom they had an emotional connection. Sex was spoken of as simply a physical act with any willing female. Since there was no emotional (romantic) association with having sex, having multiple sex partners, even though they might have a girlfriend, was not seen as wrong or cheating.

General perception that falling pregnant while still at school was not acceptable

Specifically voiced by girls the opinions were very strong in this regard. The reaction of shock and anger by all parents of the girls included in the case studies showed that teenage pregnancy had not been normalised in these communities, although most girls did receive a certain level of support from their parents once the baby was born.

The social environment of learners

According to the learners the five aspects that impacted on their lives the most were: teenage pregnancy; rape/forced sex; alcohol abuse; violence and crime; and emotional abuse. These issues were not mentioned in detail in our conversations with learners. The five top aspects rated by the learners as having some effect on their lives were: alcohol abuse; lack of safety at school; peer pressure; lack of recreational activities; and lack of parental support.

General sanctioning of negative social behaviour

On the whole learners sanctioned negative behaviour, showing that they had a clear concept of what was considered unacceptable and what was deemed appropriate social behaviour.

Risky behaviour as a product of emotional stress experienced by teenagers

According to learners from both schools the engaging of teenagers in high-risk behaviour could be attributed to the stress experienced by teenagers resulting from their home environments (broken families) and a lack of parental and adult authority in the household and communities. Teenagers were described by adults (in interviews with parents) as having a total disregard for adult authority with a strong rebellion against submission to such authority.

Moving towards an intervention programme: Aspects to consider

The 2010 Cochrane review on interventions for preventing unintended pregnancies among adolescents (Oringanje *et al.*, 2009), mentions three important aspects for intervention programmes to be successful:

1. interventions that are designed to reduce teen pregnancies appear to be most effective when a **multifaceted approach** is used, as the problem is multiple determined and multidimensional;
2. interventions **should not only focus on sexual factors** and related consequences, but should also include non-sexual factors such as skills training and personal development;
3. stakeholders including teens, parents, health sector, schools and churches **should work together to devise programmes** that are

practical, evidence based, culturally appropriate and acceptable to the target population.

Jewkes *et al.* (2009) mention further that the *power relations within relationships* and how choices are negotiated by both teenage girls and boys are very important:

> Implicit in this is an understanding that teenage pregnancy is not just an issue of reproductive health and young women's bodies, but, rather, one, in its causes and consequences that is rooted in women's gendered social environment.

Gender power inequalities overlap with other dimensions to teenagers' power, including: socio-economic status; education; social skills and confidence; and age-related social status.

In general the ability of teenagers to make decisions on their sexuality and prevent unwanted pregnancy (or not want a pregnancy) depended to a large extent on their ability to control their environment and access resources.

Furthermore the threat and experience of sexual and physical violence were particular barriers to young women's ability to practise safe sexual behaviours (including discussing HIV, remaining abstinent or using condoms) given power imbalances between young women and their partners. Programmes to reduce adolescent pregnancies and HIV risk in South Africa and elsewhere in sub-Saharan Africa must address sexual violence as part of effective prevention strategies (Speizer *et al.*, 2009).

With reference to unequal relationships, interventions to reduce teenage pregnancy **need to focus on both men and women**. Men have particularly been left out of the equation, yet very commonly women become pregnant as teenagers because their male partner wants them to and makes it very difficult for them to resist.

The importance of the **school environment and school attachment** has also been mentioned as essential in preventing teenage pregnancies in a number of ways.

When teenagers feel a sense of attachment or connection to school and are successful at school, they are less likely to fall pregnant. School attachment, academic achievement and higher aspirations for education offer incentives to teenagers to avoid pregnancy

(Kirby, 2002). According to the South African Department of Health (2003), pregnancy rates decrease with increasing education – 20% of 15–19-year-old women with a grade 6–7 education, and only 7% with a higher education, reported having been pregnant. The causes of teenage pregnancy are complex, and are (among other things) influenced by household poverty, access to information and contraception, the nature of gender relations and the often unequal decision-making power between men and women relationships. However **pregnancy is often the end results of a process of alienation from schooling and a complex set of other social issues, rather than the cause of drop-out** (Strassburg *et al.*, 2010a).

Promoting school attachment may decrease learner's engagement in risky behaviour. School attachment is related to a range of factors such as school climate, overall sense of safety, structured social integration (e.g. sport activities), extra-curricular activities, peer relations, teacher support, school/class room leadership and management (including learners active involvement) and a sense of belonging (Strassburg *et al.*, 2010b).

In the light of our findings in the research, as well as findings derived from the literature on prevention of teenage pregnancies, it is clear that the following three areas should be focused on as first steps towards a long-term intervention in the region:

1. **The learners**
   a. reproductive health;
   b. mental health;
   c. asset building programmes.

2. **The school**
   a. after-school activities;
   b. programmes to stimulate interest and loyalty towards school;
   c. school to become a place of safety and support.

3. **The parents**
   a. parenting programmes for young parents as well as parents of learners;
   b. mothers as well as fathers included;

    c.   create and strengthen communication and trust between parents and learners.

Conclusion

Teenage pregnancy is regarded as a risk factor for the disruption of education, future employment, sexually transmitted diseases, HIV, pre-term birth and poor mental health. The pregnant teenager is consequently rendered more vulnerable to poverty, exploitative sexual relations and violence. It is therefore crucial to try to understand the perceptions and attitudes of teenagers regarding teenage pregnancy as well as to explore their understanding of sexuality and contraception. The purpose of this chapter has been: firstly to give a description of the social and home environment of teenagers in two secondary schools in a rural, wine-producing area in South Africa: and secondly to try to understand, through in-depth interviews with teenagers (including father- and mother-learners), their decision-making processes and attitudes regarding sexual activity and pregnancies. Important information was gathered and it became clear that any intervention aimed at addressing high-risk behaviour should focus on an asset-building approach, which will result in higher resilience and in an informed youth.

References

Anderson, B. A. (2003) 'Fertility, poverty and gender in South Africa', Paper 2 in *Fertility: The Current South African Issues of Poverty, HIV/AIDS and Youth*, Pretoria: Child, Youth and Family Development Research Programme, Human Sciences Research Council. Available from www.hsrc.ac.za/en/research-data/view/1057 (accessed 27 June 2016)

Clarke, C. L., Rhynas, S., Schwannauer, M. and Taylor, J. (2016) 'Advancing risk and resilience – why is it so important?', in Clarke, C. L., Rhynas, S., Schwannauer, M. and Taylor, J. (eds) (2016) *Risk and Resilience: Global learning across the age span*, Edinburgh, Dunedin Academic Press

Department of Education (2007) 'Measures for the prevention and management of learner pregnancy' (online). Available from URL: www.naptosa.org.za/index.php/doc-manager/40-professional/46-general/105-sgb-dbe-pregnancy-2007/file (accessed 27 June 2016)

Department of Health (1999) *Summary Report: 1998 national HIV sero-prevalence survey of women attending public antenatal clinics in South Africa*, Pretoria: Health Systems Research and Epidemiology, Department of Health

Department of Health (2001) *National Contraception Policy Guidelines within a Reproductive Health Framework*, Pretoria: Department of Health

Department of Health (2003) *National Contraceptive Services Delivery Guide-*

lines, Pretoria: Department of Health

Ehlers, V. J. (2003) 'Psychological impact of teenage pregnancy on pregnant teenagers', *Journal on School of Social Sciences*, Vol. 11, No. 13, pp. 307–13

Holborn, L. and Eddy, G. (2011) *First Steps to Healing the South African Family*, Johannesburg: South African Institute of Race Relations

Jewkes, R., Morrell, R. and Christofides, N. (2009) 'Empowering teenagers to prevent pregnancy: Lessons from South Africa', *Culture, Health and Sexuality*, Vol. 11, No. 7, pp. 675–88

Kirby, D. (2002) 'Antecedents of adolescent initiation of sex, contraceptive use, and pregnancy', *American Journal of Health Behavior*, Vol. 26, No. 6, pp. 473–85(13)

Moultrie, T. A. and Timæus, I. M. (2003) 'The South African fertility decline: Evidence from two censuses and a demographic and health survey', *Population Studies*, Vol. 57, No. 3, pp. 265–83

National Population Unit (2000) *The State of South Africa's Population Report*, Pretoria: Department of Social Development

Oringanje, C., Meremikwu, M. M., Eko, H., Esu, E., Meremikwu, A. and Ehiri, J. E. (2009) 'Interventions for preventing unintended pregnancies among adolescents', *Cochrane Database Syst Rev.*, Vol. 4, CD005215; doi: 10.1002/14651858.CD005215.pub2.

Speizer, I. S., Pettifor, A., Cummings, S., MacPhail, C., Kleinschmidt, I. and Rees, H. V. (2009) 'Sexual violence and reproductive health outcomes among South African female youths: A contextual analysis', *American Journal of Public Health*, Supplement 2, 99(S2)

Statistics South Africa (2008) *Recorded Live Births 2007*, Statistical Release P0305, Pretoria: Statistics South Africa

Statistics South Africa (2015) *Recorded Live Births, 2013*, Statistical Release P0305, Pretoria: Statistics South Africa

Strassburg, S., Meny-Gibert, S. and Russell, B. (2010a) *Left Unfinished: Temporary absence and drop out from South African Schools*, Access to Education Series, Vol. 2, Johannesburg: Social Surveys Africa

Strassburg, S., Meny-Gibert, S. and Russell, B. (2010b) *More Than Getting through the School Gates: Barriers to participation in schooling*, Access to Education Series, Vol. 3, Johannesburg: Social Surveys Africa

CHAPTER 9

Support, Protection and Citizenship: The case of people living with dementia in Sweden

Ann-Charlotte Nedlund and Annika Taghizadeh Larsson

Ann-Charlotte Nedlund and Annika Taghizadeh Larsson, Linköping University, Sweden

Introduction

Focusing on Sweden, this chapter will provide knowledge on various challenges inherent in how to protect and also support people to enhance their citizenship. The chapter will describe and discuss tensions between legal intentions that are in play in the case of older adults in need of support to make decisions in Sweden and how issues of self-determination, agency and independence, risk and safety are managed in practice in different contexts and by different actors:

> '... more and more of us are challenging boundaries and finding our voice. We are "claiming full citizenship" – speaking up and speaking out, and assuming our place at the table as capable and active participants' (Mann, 2015)

This quote by Jim Mann, an advocate, living with Alzheimer's, captures very nicely the core of maintaining self-agency and independence in a context in which the dominant perspective has been influenced by a biomedical rationale. Regrettably this is often still the case, with people living with dementia often being identified by their diagnosis or as sufferers – a matter criticised by several scholars (such as Bartlett and O'Connor, 2010; Nedlund and Nordh, 2015).

Background

An important part of claiming full citizenship is to be acknowledged as an independent individual with rights as well as an actor in society. This is also valid for people with dementia. On an international level, this need is acknowledged in the United Nations Convention on the Rights of People with Disabilities (CRPD), stating that all 'parties shall take appropriate measures to provide access by people with disabilities to the support they may require in exercising their legal capacity' (United Nations, 2006, Article 12).

However the issue of supporting people with cognitive impairments to claim and exercise their rights as citizens is legally constructed differently in different legal systems. In Sweden people with dementia are formally considered independent individuals with the same rights as other adult citizens and as actors in the society. That is, all adults have a right to self-determination, which is strongly emphasised in law, regulations and policies. Furthermore adult citizens cannot be declared as incompetent to make decisions and their right of self-determination cannot legally be taken away. Consequently matters of supported decision-making are largely unregulated (Nedlund and Taghizadeh Larsson, 2016b). This is also the case for people living with dementia, which means that Sweden differs from many other countries in how issues of supported decision-making and cognitive impairments are legally constructed. In other countries such as England, Wales, Scotland and Canada capacity assessments are prescribed in law, and defining adult people assessed as lacking decision-making capacity as non-fully capable citizens is considered as a form of protection. For example, the Mental Capacity Act (MCA) 2005 in England and Wales (Department for Constitutional Affairs, 2007) seeks to empower people as long as they maintain capacity and protect them when they lack capacity to make a certain decision (Boyle, 2008). According to the MCA, 'a person's capacity must be assessed specifically in terms of their capacity to make a particular decision at the time it needs to be made' (Department for Constitutional Affairs, 2007, p. 40). In Swedish legislation the challenges in allowing people with dementia the greatest possible freedom – while at the same time preventing harm to them, as clearly stated in the MCA – are subordinate to the issue of self-determination. This highlights that diverse welfare systems encompass different ideas about how to support and protect people with cognitive impairments.

In this chapter we describe and discuss tensions between legal intentions that are in play in the case of older adults in need of support to make decisions in Sweden and how issues of self-determination, agency and independence, risk and safety are managed in practice in different contexts and by different actors. The purpose is to provide knowledge on various challenges inherent in how to protect and support people to enhance their citizenship. The data presented here are drawn from an ongoing project 'Democracy, autonomy and justice – Citizenship practice for people with dementia' funded by the Swedish government agency FORTE – The Swedish Research Council for Health, Working Life and Welfare. The purpose of the project is to explore the citizenship content for people with dementia by disentangling how people with dementia have been portrayed both in policy documents and in policy practices by people working in welfare-state institutions and how these inform what will become the citizenship content for people with dementia. In the project the main data source is documents from national and local level combined with interviews with social workers, senior administrators and locally elected politicians in four local authorities. In this chapter we present data from the nineteen interviews with social workers/care-managers merely to illustrate the challenges and practical constraints of a legal system that addresses how to manage risk and safety in practice.

The dominance of self-determination in Sweden

The right to self-determination is central to Swedish democracy and its welfare state, and is protected and highly emphasised in Swedish legislation. The Swedish welfare state is based on an assumption of active citizens that presupposes that everyone, including people living with dementia, can assimilate information, participate in public reasoning and formulate their voice in meetings with welfare-state institutions. This idea is clearly visible in the final report by the Government Commission on 'a sustainable democracy' (SOU, 2000, p. 1): 'Every social group should be involved in [formulating] the politics, it should not be formed by a few meanwhile others are excluded.' Self-determination is also clearly highlighted in the Social Services Act (SSA) portal section that states that the work in social services 'should be based on respect for people self-determination and integrity' (SFS, 2001, p. 453). Moreover, in order to receive social care (e.g. special housing and home-care services), an application must come from the person in need of the services, that is, in this case the person living with dementia. Furthermore, care and/or support can formally be provided only if the person in need of the services has given her/his consent.

People living with dementia as independent citizens

Thus in Sweden, in law and regulations, people with dementia have the same right to self-determination as other citizens and cannot be declared as incompetent to make decisions. The assumption that active citizens, including frail and disabled people, can participate in public debate and make their case in meetings with welfare institutions is a basic premise. However, since living with dementia implies increasing cognitive as well as communicative impairments, people with dementia are vulnerable and in need of support in order to take charge of their rights and realise full citizenship. This causes a paradox. On the one hand it is of course important to acknowledge that everyone is covered by human rights and ideas of equality and is allowed to participate in decisions concerning their own life. On the other hand there is a potential risk that the dominant idea of self-determination weakens vulnerable citizens' positions, potential and opportunity to find and to have voice. For these citizens it could, in some cases, be critical to have someone else who expresses and voices their concerns.

How is protection organised in the Swedish welfare system?

In order to protect vulnerable adult citizens there are two forms of representatives available in Sweden: Special Representative (in Swedish *Godmanskap* meaning 'God man') and Legal Administrator (in Swedish *Förvaltarskap* and/or *Förvaltare*). Another legal institution that can be used is the power of attorney (in Swedish *Fullmakt*; the English terminology is taken from the Swedish national courts administration).

Several actors are involved in legally securing these different forms of representatives. The social services authority is not allowed to represent people but is obliged to notify the *Municipal Board of Chief Guardians* (in Swedish 'Överförmyndarenhete') if they consider that the person is in need of a Special Representative or Legal Administrator (SALAR, 2011). The district court (in Swedish 'Tingsrätt') appoints the Special Representative or Legal Administrator, but it is the role of the Municipal Board of Chief Guardians to investigate the need for a Special Representative or Legal Administrator. As a rule the Municipal Board of Chief Guardians turns to the responsible unit of social service for details on the individual's needs. The Municipal Board of Chief Guardians is also responsible for the supervision of Special Representative or Legal Administrator. The County Administrative Boards (in Swedish *Länsstyrelsen*) have a supervising role for the Municipal Board of Chief Guardians and also support Chief Guardians in promoting the law (SOU, 2013).

The Special Representative can assist the person in making decisions and in protecting rights and interests, concerning issues such as private finances and adequate care provision. By representing without depriving the person's autonomy and right to self-determination, the Special Representative is an internationally unique arrangement and is based on the idea that every adult citizen should have equal rights regardless of her/his decision-making capacity (SALAR, 2011). In order to be appointed a Special Representative, it is required that the person (legally called as the principal) has a medical condition that entails a need for support in, for example, payments of bills and taking care of things that she or he owns. In principle the person in question should consent to have a Special Representative, but if there is a medical record consent is not always necessary. A so-called Full Special Representative consists of three parts: managing the property owned by the person in need; protecting his or her rights; and providing for her or him as a person. The form of Special Representatives is based on the principle of least intrusive measure, which means that the Special Representative should be appointed only if the person's needs cannot be met in any other way (SALAR, 2011).

The same is true for a Legal Administrator. However the Legal Administrator is a coercive measure by the welfare state and can, unlike the Special Representative, be enforced by the district court against the person's will. Whoever gets a Legal Administrator loses every right to act in 'what the administration encompasses' (c.f. SALAR, 2011). A person who has a Legal Administrator must have the consent of the administrator to conclude contracts and the Legal Administrator has sole control of the property subject to the administration. Thus a Legal Administrator can be regarded as a formal form of substitute decision-maker covering financial and property matters. Important to note is that neither Special Representatives nor Legal Administrators have a legal right to decide on most issues concerning healthcare and social services, particularly not in long-term cases (SOU, 2015, p. 80).

Power of attorney (regulated in the Contracts Act; SFS, 1915, p. 218) is another form of legal institution that can be used when making decisions on behalf of someone. However power of attorney is legally applicable only in cases in which individuals retain their capacity; consequently they do not – legally speaking – apply to people with decision-making incapacity or in cases where a person's decision-making is considered as inadequate (Rynning, 1994; SOU, 2004, p. 112; SOU, 2015, p. 80).

Moreover, in Sweden, family members or next of kin have no legal authority to act against the will of the individual in issues concerning health and long-term care. Nor do relatives or friends have any legal authority to act as surrogates or to consent to healthcare, social care and long-term care against the individual's will (Ministry of Health and Social Affairs, 2012). The role of the authority of social services is also limited. According to Swedish Social Affairs (SSA), the Ministry of Health and Social Affairs and the MCA concerning support and services for people with certain functional impairments (SFS, 1993, p. 387), support and services may be granted upon request and according to needs, but shall not be provided against the person's will.

Thus in the Swedish welfare-state system there are a number of legal arrangements that to varying degrees protect and compensate for the vulnerability of people and support people with decision-making incapacity. However there is no arrangement that gives someone the right to decide for a person living with dementia about healthcare and/or social care services, except in cases of momentary emergency, which are covered by the 'rule of necessity' in the Code of Penalty (SFS, 1962, p. 700; see also the Patient Act – SFS, 2014, p. 821 – and the Compulsory Mental Care Act – SFS, 1991, p. 1,128), but then such decisions cannot be ruled for long.

So what happens in practice? How to get support and how to protect?

As a consequence of how issues of representing and protecting people with dementia are legally constructed and organised in Sweden, with self-determination as the dominant idea, a clear dilemma arises in practice, particularly in relation to social care and long-term care (c.f. Österholm *et al.*, 2015; Nedlund and Taghi-zadeh Larsson, 2016a; Nordh and Nedlund, 2015). As we have seen, on the one hand, according to the law, the right to self-determination of the person as a citizen has to be respected in every single case except in an emergency. On the other hand, people with dementia may have cognitive and communication disabilities that make it difficult for them to express needs and wishes, to make decisions and to remember agreements they have made.

Accordingly, in practice, it is a matter of fact that people living with dementia often have difficulties with independent self-determination. As one care-manager reflects on her experiences of assessment meetings with someone living with dementia:

> 'It's hard for them because they [people with dementia] are not always aware of what we talk about at this moment right here, and then you've been sitting in a meeting, agreed upon ... that they [home-care services] will come every morning, and then they [people with dementia] can call us the next morning and tell us that they haven't ordered any help.'
> (Care-manager Sara)

Another care-manager explains that it is common for people with dementia to present a social facade by picturing themselves as having more capacity than they really have:

> 'One can sound really adequate when you visit someone who has this diagnosis. "Do you need help with going for

walks? "No no no. I've just been out, I came in right now, I've been walking," but they haven't been out walking …' (Care-manager Anna)

Besides the difficulties of self-determination and agreement, the examples above also illustrate the sometimes limited knowledge by others of how it is to live with dementia. This can, for example, be related to the first quote above, when it is necessary to understand that for a person who has dementia and its impairments some days can be better than others. One way to promote safety is to raise awareness of dementia – and to challenge the biomedical rationale and to foster a more inclusive perspective – among the public and also among the professionals encountering people with dementia.

Besides care-managers, people living with dementia and their relatives, those who have to deal with this problematic situation in practice are: public servants (working at different levels in the public administration and with various professional background); Special Representatives; and Legal Administrators. These actors have to consider and handle competing demands: to follow the law and rules; to be loyal to superiors and others in the organisation; to consider their professional knowledge; and to respect and – if needed – to protect vulnerable individual citizens (Nedlund, 2012). Every day they handle real-life situations, meeting people with various conditions, where they have to handle these pressure and judge what to do in each situation. Their handling of ethical dilemmas relies on professional judgement and experience and goes far beyond formal regulation (Lipsky, 2010; Wagenaar, 2011; Nedlund, 2012).

According to legislation, the care-manager cannot decide on services if the person does not want to apply for them or to receive them. In that case an important strategy to encourage consent and implicitly weigh up risk turns into one of persuasion by 'coaxing' (Nordh and Nedlund, 2015), which is expressed by one care-manager:

'… then one has to coax in order for them to apply, since they don't want to apply for anything'. (Care-manager Jenny)

In this grey area of ideas and practice the various actors have to find creative ways to ensure that they receive consent. One care-manager describes this dilemma and her creative way of handling it:

> '... sometimes we give support even if the person explicitly says "no", we do that since there's some kind of paragraph of necessity ... I think, I don't know where exactly, but ... but if it's obvious that the person doesn't eat, for example, and that you see that that's the case, it could be that we make an order to the home services to leave a food box on the door, and if it's gone the next day or so, one could interpret that it's some kind of consent.' (Care-manager Karin)

So as we can see it can sometimes be difficult as a care-manager to know how to support the individual effectively. It is a tough task to balance these different pressures. Clients' needs and situations vary and in real-life cases different pressures can interact and even conflict with each other: for example, the right to self-determina-tion and informed consent versus the need to protect – and not to risk – the individual's physical well-being and life. Professionals experience particular challenges when the law does not take full account of the reality of daily practice. A welfare system that is responsible for protecting its citizens but is based on the premise that every citizen should participate independently in decision-making undoubtedly raises issues for those citizens who lack deci-sion-making capacity. The issue has the characteristics of a 'wicked problem' characterised by its uncertainty and ambiguity (Rittel and Webber, 1973; also Schön and Rein, 1994) and therefore by its lack of guidance of what to do and how to work and act. This leads to considerable variation in the actual interactions between people living with dementia and representatives of the welfare-state institutions.

Moreover it also implies that people with dementia, to a large extent, depend on the intentions of the people around them and hence are vulnerable to 'risky situations'. This dependence on others is not protected in law as the legal system does not recog-nise such dependence; in other words, it is legally constructed as a 'non-occurring matter' that should not happen. One such risky situation, as one care-managers explains, is that often people with dementia are under great pressure from their relatives:

> 'I think that many times they [people with dementia] are under great pressure from the relatives. They say something when the relatives are present and something else when I talk to them on my own … the person agrees upon almost everything just so that the meeting should end. When the meeting ends and even before I, or a relative, hardly have left, they [people with dementia] call and tell me that they don't want anything, they will not accept help.' (Care-manager Agneta)

What becomes even more difficult in practice is that there are no specific rules or guidelines for how the different actors should reason or act when they make decisions for a person with adjustments or support needs, except that decisions should be made with the person's best interest in mind. This can be compared with countries such as England and Wales where the Mental Capacity Act 2005 also enshrines decision-making in an individual's best interests but also details the sorts of information and considerations that the representative, guardian or substitute should – and should not – take into consideration in their decision-making (Department for Constitutional Affairs, 2007).

As we have seen, to claim the right of social care the person has to know the social care system's functions. In other words, a person living with dementia has to know how to apply, what to apply for and where to apply for services. Also the application has to be made by the person her(him)self.

A way forward?

So, what is the way forward? The quote at the beginning of this chapter by Jim Mann (2015) guides us on how to respond to the large group of people with dementia who are fully able, but not always allowed, to make independent decisions about their own life and future. To be acknowledged as a citizen is to be assumed 'as capable and active participant', it is about 'finding the voice', 'speaking up and speaking out' – in other words to maintain self-agency. Protection by the welfare state, to have this freedom, risks to imply limitations of getting one's voice heard and further to be acknowledged as independent and retain self-agency if you cannot speak up for yourself and if there is no one who legally can judge that you require protection. Also, protection by the welfare state, where it is judged that a citizen requires help and thus limitation of freedom, could also be a risk and imply the same kind of limitations. Thus it is complicated to limit the autonomy and self-determination of adults by legislation. There are many considerations of balance: between freedom and security; between the welfare state's responsibility and obligation to protect vulnerable individuals and social groups versus limiting autonomy and self-determination; and between consent and constraint. Yet another challenge is between having general and flexible rules or more rigid rules where the former gives a scope for individually designed support and for taking into account the person's circumstances and capacity to make decisions, to take charge of their rights and consider their interests.

However, as we have shown in this chapter by illustrating the situation in Sweden, it is also complicated when the self-determination of some people is not limited, and this might be considered as a way of transferring difficult dilemmas concerning support, protection, risk and citizenship to the actual encounters between vulnerable people and e.g. public servants. Without any formal guidance, public servants are currently handling tensions concerning independence, and right to self-determination vis-à-vis the need to step in and make decisions not only on behalf of but also instead of a person in the later stages of dementia. Apart from a few studies, very little is known about the practice of substitute decision-making for those living with dementia by public servants in Sweden. There is also the possibility of variation between and within various authorities. Furthermore, since the legal systems differ in different countries (Boyle, 2008; Sokolowski, 2010), it cannot be assumed that international research in this field is transferable to Swedish settings.

Furthermore, as has been pointed out in other chapters of this book, the policy shift from a societal and comprehensive welfare-state responsibility to an individual, and in some case to family, makes these vulnerable citizens even more dependent on personal circumstances such as if they have people around who have their best interests in mind.

Accordingly, what we can see here are the challenges inherent between how to protect and how to support people with decision-making incapacity in order to enhance their citizenship – conflicting matters that we can find both in legal regulations and in practice.

Conclusion

This chapter has covered matters concerning how, when and by whom and on what grounds voices of people with dementia should be supported and in some cases substituted – matters that ultimately encompass the tensions that are inconsistent in the welfare system's responsibility to protect its citizens versus the individual citizen's right to be independent, self-managing and with a right to self-determination. In concrete experiences, it is about matters that become clear in the course of life-changing decision-making and vital personal choices: for example, who should decide about a move to residential home, as well as in more minor daily and iterative decisions about what clothes a person should wear, and when and what she will have for dinner. An important starting point for the chapter has been to consider the individual's interaction and exposure both with personal experiences and with the perspectives of legal institutions considering how support, protection and self-determination should be managed – conditions that may vary in time and space.

A way forward would be, in our view, to acknowledge people living with dementia's place at the table and the need to support their influence on their own lives as well as their citizenship. What we have seen is that societies have different options and they can adapt any choice over the course of time. The chapter could be the basis of more informed reflections and political decisions about how to proceed in order to support people with dementia to claim and exercise their citizenship.

References

Bartlett, R. and O'Connor, D. (2010) *Broadening the Dementia Debate: Towards social citizenship*, Bristol: Policy Press

Boyle, G. (2008) 'The Mental Capacity Act 2005: Promoting the citizenship of people with dementia?', *Health and Social Care in the Community*, Vol. 16,

No. 5, pp. 529–37

Department for Constitutional Affairs (2007) *Mental Capacity Act 2005. Code of Practice*, London: Stationery Office

Lipsky, M. (2010) *Street-Level Bureaucracy: Dilemmas of the individual in public services*, New York, NY: Sage

Mann, Jim (2015), in *Claiming Full Citizenship: Self-Determination, Personalization, Individualized Funding*, conference brochure, 2015 International Conference, 15–17 October 2015, The Hyatt Regency, Vancouver, Canada. Available from http://interprofessional.ubc.ca/ClaimingFullCitizenship2015/brochure.pdf (accessed 5 May 2016)

Ministry of Health and Social Affairs (2012) *God vård och omsorg om personer med demenssjukdom samt regler för skydd och rättssäkerhet*, Lagrådsremiss: Socialdepartementet

Nedlund, A.-C. (2012) *Designing for Legitimacy: Policy work and the art of juggling when setting limits in health care*, Linköping: Department of Medical and Health Sciences, Linköping University

Nedlund, A.-C. and Nordh, J. (2015) 'Crafting citizen(ship) for people with dementia: How policy narratives at national level in Sweden informed politics of time from 1975 to 2013', *Journal of Aging Studies*, Vol. 34, pp. 123–33

Nedlund, A.-C. and Taghizadeh Larsson, A. (2016a) 'To protect and to support: How citizenship and self-determination is legally constructed and managed in practice for people living with dementia in Sweden', *Dementia*, Vol. 15, No. 3, pp. 343–57

Nedlund, A.-C. and Taghizadeh Larsson, A. (2016b) 'Ställföreträdarskap och självbestämmande' in Hellström, I. and Hydén, L.-C. (2016) *Att Leva med Demens*, Malmö: Gleerups

Nordh, J. and Nedlund, A.-C. (2016) 'To Coordinate Information in Practice: Dilemmas and Strategies in Care Management for Citizens with Dementia', *Journal of Social Service Research*, DOI: 10.1080/01488376.2016.1217580 .

Österholm, H. J., Taghizadeh Larsson, A. and Olaison, A. (2015) 'Handling the dilemma of self-determination and dementia: A study of case managers' discursive strategies in assessment meetings', *Journal of Gerontological Social Work*, Vol. 58, No. 6, pp. 613–36

Rittel, H. and Webber, M. (1973) 'Dilemmas in a general theory of planning', *Policy Sciences*, Vol. 4, pp. 155–69

Rynning, E. (1994) *Samtycke till medicinsk vård och behandling. En rättsvetenskaplig studie*, Uppsala: Justus

SALAR (2011) *Socialnämndens anmälningsskyldighet I frågor som rör god man, förvaltare samt visa vårdnads- och förmynderskapsfrågor cirkulär 2011:35*, Stockholm: Swedish Association of Local Authorities and Regions [Sveriges kommuner och landsting]

Schön, D. A. and Rein, M. (1994) *Frame Reflection: Toward the resolution of intractable policy controversies*, New York, NY: Basic Books

SFS (1915) *Contracts Act* [Lag om avtal och andra rättshandlingar på förmögenhetsrättens område], 1915:218 Swedish Code of Statutes [Svensk författningssamling]

SFS (1962) *The Code of Penalty* [Brottsbalken], 1962:700 Swedish Code of Statutes [Svensk författningssamling]

SFS (1991) *Mental Care Act* [Lag om psykiatrisk tvångsvård], 1991:1128 Swedish Code of Statutes [Svensk författningssamling]

SFS (1993) *Act Concerning Support and Service for Persons with Certain Functional Impairment* [Lag om stöd och service till visa funktionshindrade], 1993:387 Swedish Code of Statutes [Svensk författningssamling]

SFS (2001) *The Social Services Act* [Socialtjänstlagen], 2001:453 Swedish Code of Statutes [Svensk författningssamling]

SFS (2014) *The Patient Act* [Patientlagen], 2014:821 Swedish Code of Statutes [Svensk författningssamling]

Sokolowski, M. (2010) 'Advance directives and the problem of informed consent', *Journal of Ethics in Mental Health*, Vol. 5, pp. 1–6

SOU (2000) *Demokratiutredningens betänkande: En uthållig demokrati! Politik för folkstyrelse på 2000- talet* [A sustainable democracy: Politics for democracy in the 21st century: Final report from the Democracy Commission], Swedish Official Government Reports 2000:1 [Statens offentliga utredningar]. Stockholm: Fritzes

SOU (2004) *Frågor om ställföreträdare och förmyndare för vuxna*, Swedish Official Government Reports 2004:112 [Statens offentliga utredningar], Stockholm: Fritzes

SOU (2013) *Vissa frågor om godemän och förvaltare.* Betänkande av Utredningen om bättre förutsättningar för godemän ochf örvaltare, Swedish Official Government Reports [Statens offentliga utredningar] 2013:27, Stockholm: Fritzes

SOU (2015) *Stöd och hjälp till vuxna vid ställningstaganden till vård, omsorg och forskning*, Swedish Official Government Reports [Statens offentliga utredningar] 2015:80, Stockholm: Fritzes

United Nations (2006) *Convention on the Rights of Persons with Disabilities* (CRPD), New York, NY: United Nations. Available from URL: www.un.org/disabilities/documents/convention/convoptprot-e.pdf

Wagenaar, H. (2011) *Meaning in Action: Interpretation and dialogue in policy analysis*, Armonk, NY: Sharpe

INDEX

Note: page numbers in *italics* denote figures or tables